Essential Histories

The Napoleonic Wars

The Peninsular War 1807–1814

Essential Histories

The Napoleonic Wars

The Peninsular War 1807–1814

Gregory Fremont-Barnes

First published in Great Britain in 2002 by Osprey Publishing,
Elms Court, Chapel Way, Botley, Oxford OX2 9LP
Email: info@ospreypublishing.com

ISBN 1 84176 370 5

Editor: Rebecca Cullen
Design: Ken Vail Graphic Design, Cambridge, UK
Cartography by The Map Studio
Index by Alan Thatcher
Picture research by Image Select International
Origination by Grasmere Digital Imaging, Leeds, UK
Printed and bound in China by L. Rex Printing Company Ltd.

02 03 04 05 06   10 9 8 7 6 5 4 3 2 1

For a complete list of titles available from Osprey Publishing
please contact:

Osprey Direct UK, PO Box 140,
Wellingborough, Northants, NN8 4ZA, UK.
Email: info@ospreydirect.co.uk

Osprey Direct USA,
c/o Motorbooks International, PO Box 1,
Osceola, WI 54020-0001, USA.
Email: info@ospreydirectusa.com

www.ospreypublishing.com

This book is one of four volumes on the The Napoleonic Wars
in the Osprey Essential Histories series

Author's note: Readers should be aware that Spanish and
Portuguese place names have varied over time and sometimes
assume different spellings when anglicized. Thus, one encounters:
'Bailen' and 'Baylen', 'Bussaco' and 'Busaco', 'Vitoria' and 'Vittoria'
and so on. With no definitive agreement among military
historians on this problem, this work has therefore adopted the
most commonly-used forms.

Contents

Introduction

In 1807 Napoleon stood at the height of his power, having defeated every major European power except Britain, who resolutely refused to abandon the struggle against an unbeaten and, apparently, unbeatable foe. Circumstances were soon to change, however. Napoleon's decision to occupy the Iberian Peninsula resulted in a long and costly war to which, at long last, Britain could make a substantial contribution on land. Napoleon graphically described the Peninsular War as his 'Spanish ulcer'. This bitter seven-year struggle, which began in Portugal, then expanded into Spain and ended in southern France, relentlessly consumed vast numbers of men and equally vast quantities of equipment and money. The peninsula from which the war takes its name, the Iberian Peninsula, was the sole theater of operations, but the fact that the Peninsular War was restricted to Spain and Portugal should not disguise the importance of the conflict in the greater context of the Napoleonic Wars. On the contrary, the campaigns fought across the length and breadth of the peninsula played a significant part in the ultimate downfall of Napoleon and therefore rightfully form together a distinctive and crucial phase of the many wars waged against him.

Napoleon could not have foreseen in 1807 the significance of the Peninsular War, however wise we have become with the benefit of hindsight. Nor was it by any means clear that, when the French invaded Portugal in that year, what had begun as an operation to close her ports to British trade would quickly develop into a major conflict that would rapidly involve not simply the forces of Portugal and France, but those of Spain and Britain as well.

Napoleon's lightning campaigns of 1805–1807 were based on a system that relied on rapid march and concentration of force. The army lived off the land rather than being dependent on lengthy supply lines, cumbersome commissariat wagons and static depots. In short, his armies fed themselves on the move, and maximum force could thus be concentrated at a desired point. However, Napoleon's experiences in east Prussia and Poland in the first half of 1807 had shown how difficult it was to conduct operations when laboring under the twin disadvantages of poor land and roads. The Iberian Peninsula had both these disadvantages. The *Grande Armée* could sustain itself under such conditions for a limited period – but not for years on end. Extreme poverty, primitive communications by road – in many cases merely a shabby dirt track – unnavigable rivers, and forbidding mountain ranges created formidable obstacles to large bodies of men and horses.

The problems experienced by the French were greatly exacerbated by the fact that they faced not only the regular armed forces of the Allies, but also the ordinary peoples of the Iberian peninsula themselves. As Clausewitz put it a few years later: 'In Spain the war became of itself an affair of the people …' Ordinary French soldiers like Albert de Rocca, a veteran of many campaigns, captured the essence of the kind of fanatical resistance that he and his comrades faced:

We were not called to fight against [professional] troops … but against a people insulated from all the other continental nations by its manners, its prejudices, and even the nature of its country. The Spaniards were to oppose to us a resistance so much more the obstinate, as they believed it to be the object of the French government to make the Peninsula a secondary state, irrevocably subject to the dominion of France.

Indeed, the French soon discovered that neither the geography nor the population were at all hospitable. No conflict prior to the twentieth century posed such a daunting combination of native resistance and natural obstacles. Topographical features in Iberia ranged from the snow-capped Pyrenees to the burning wastes of the Sierra Morena. If geography and climate were not extreme enough, combatants were constantly subject to virulent diseases including typhus, dysentery, and malaria.

Napoleon's decision to occupy Spain proved a great miscalculation. Past experiences of occupation in western and central Europe were characterized, with some notable exceptions, by passive populations who submitted to French authority in general and in some cases to Bonapartist rule specifically. Spain was the only country occupied by France that Napoleon had not entirely conquered. For the Emperor, waging war against regular armies was the stuff that had made his armies legendary in their own time. However, in the Peninsula a national cause, very different from that which had so animated the French during the 1790s, but just as potent, rapidly and inexorably spread the spirit of revolt across the provinces. All across Spain's vast rural expanse, with its conspicuous absence of a large middle class, which might have acted as a moderate force, a virulent form of nationalism took firm hold. Far from embracing any liberal notions of political or social reform on the model of the French Revolution, this movement championed a cause diametrically opposed to change, with an anachronistic and almost blind faith in Crown and Church. In a society that was overwhelmingly rural, the mass of simple, ignorant peasantry held up the Bourbon monarchy as the defenders of the true faith, descendants of their forebears who had liberated medieval Spain from the hated Moors.

In short, the war became something of a crusade, but of liberation rather than conquest, and the clergy enthusiastically invoked divine help in ridding the land of occupiers whom they portrayed as agents of the Devil. Such bitter sentiments had not been seen in Europe since the dreadful days of the wars of religion in the sixteenth and seventeenth centuries. So great was the depth of feeling that even Protestant British troops were considered heretics: the Spanish even sometimes objected to the burial of those troops – their own allies – in consecrated Catholic ground. The atheistic, liberal principles of the French Revolution were seen by many reactionary Spanish nobles and clergymen as grave threats to their authority and property, to social harmony and the spiritual righteousness of the one true religion. The French became a convenient focus of attention for all Spanish society's problems, not least its grinding poverty.

The contrast between the conduct of the regular, professional forces and those of the guerrillas was remarkable. Two distinct types of war, one conventional and the other unconventional, were quickly to emerge. The British and French met in set-piece battles and skirmishes and generally treated each other with courtesy off the battlefield. In fact, fraternization was commonplace, despite Wellington's strict orders to the contrary. Provided they were observed in advance, foraging parties were generally left in peace and sentries at outposts frequently bartered goods, smoked together and chatted. Informal truces between pickets enabled each side to exchange small numbers of badly injured prisoners.

The guerrilla war, however, marked a low point in barbarity for both sides. Partisans, whose proliferation proved unstoppable, ruthlessly cut down small groups of soldiers at isolated posts, stragglers, and the wounded. French troops regularly committed atrocities in the countryside, including pillage, murder, and arson. Atrocities committed by both sides rapidly assumed an enormous scale and a horrendous nature, with reprisal feeding bloody reprisal, thus continuing the cycle of bitterness and swelling the partisan ranks. The conflict in the Peninsula, therefore, being both a clash of professional armies and a struggle involving entire peoples,

Assassination by guerrillas. With an unseen enemy constantly prowling the rugged wilderness, French sentries, stragglers, and those operating in small detachments relaxed their vigilance at their peril. Guerrilla activity cost the French well over 100,000 men – though precise figures are impossible to calculate – and placed an untold strain on the morale of those who were unharmed by these elusive and often cruel opponents. (Bacler d'Albe, Musée de l'Armée)

contained elements of both conventional and unconventional warfare, making it a precursor in many ways to the conflicts of the twentieth century.

The Peninsular War spanned most of the years of the Napoleonic Empire. When it began the Emperor of France stood triumphant over nearly the whole of the European continent. The reputation of the British Army had not yet recovered from its defeat in the War of American Independence and from its poor showing in the French Revolutionary Wars, and Sir Arthur Wellesley, the future Duke of Wellington, was only a minor general whose destiny was not yet clear. Yet in the course of the war Wellington heaped victory upon victory. By the time the war had ended, in 1814, the British Army had, despite many retreats, marched from the shores of Portugal to southern France, emerging as one of the most professional, well-motivated, and efficient fighting forces ever to have left British shores, led by the nation's greatest soldier. That the French were doomed from the start is certainly open to question; but that the Peninsular War ultimately played a critical role in the defeat of France is incontestable.

Napoleon himself acknowledged the fact years later during his exile on St. Helena when he admitted that

... that miserable Spanish affair turned opinion against me and rehabilitated England. It enabled them to continue the war. The markets of South America were opened to them; they put an army on the Peninsula ... [which] became the agent of victory, the terrible node of all the intrigues that formed on the Continent ... [the Spanish affair] is what killed me.

Iberian Peninsula, 1807

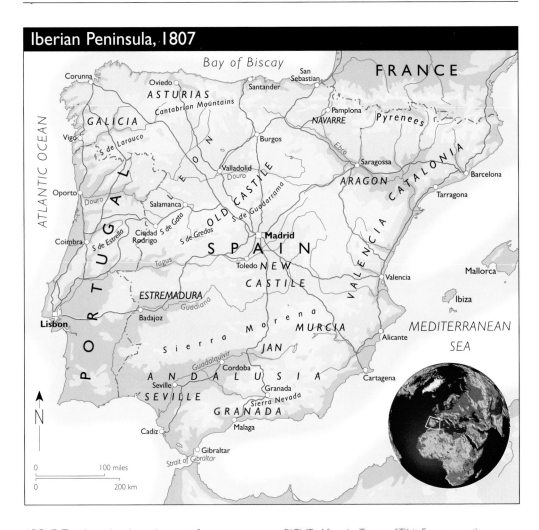

ABOVE The sheer size, dramatic range of differing geography, varying climate, and primitive roads of the Peninsula made communication between regions difficult and, in some seasons, all but impossible. Spain alone contained about 12 million people and measured about 193,000 square miles (500,000 square kilometers), including a vast central tableland. Still, it boasted many ranges several thousand feet in elevation. The Peninsula's extremely wide range of climates heavily affected campaigning: everything from temperate in the northwest to semi-arid in the south; heavy rainfall in some areas; parched landscape, where nothing can grow for months, in others. In some areas temperatures fluctuate greatly, even between night and day, and burning summers are matched by freezing winters. The south experiences both flood and drought, while on the eastern and southern coasts it is generally warm or downright hot, regularly exceeding 100 degrees F in the summer months.

RIGHT After the Treaty of Tilsit France was the dominant political and military power on the European continent, having defeated all three Continental Great Powers – Austria, Prussia, and Russia – in rapid succession, with the last now in actual alliance with her. So pervasive was France that she influenced or directly controlled territory in every direction. To the south lay her ally, Spain. To the southeast, all of mainland Italy contained states dependent on, or allied to, France, including Naples, which was ruled by Joseph Bonaparte, Napoleon's older brother. To the north, France had long since absorbed Belgium, while Louis Bonaparte ruled Holland. To the east, Switzerland was a vassal state, while in Germany the states composing the Confederation of the Rhine were all subservient to France in varying degrees, with Westphalia ruled directly by Jerome Bonaparte and Hanover (a British possession) under occupation since 1803. Far to the east, the Duchy of Warsaw was a new and staunch French ally.

Europe in 1807

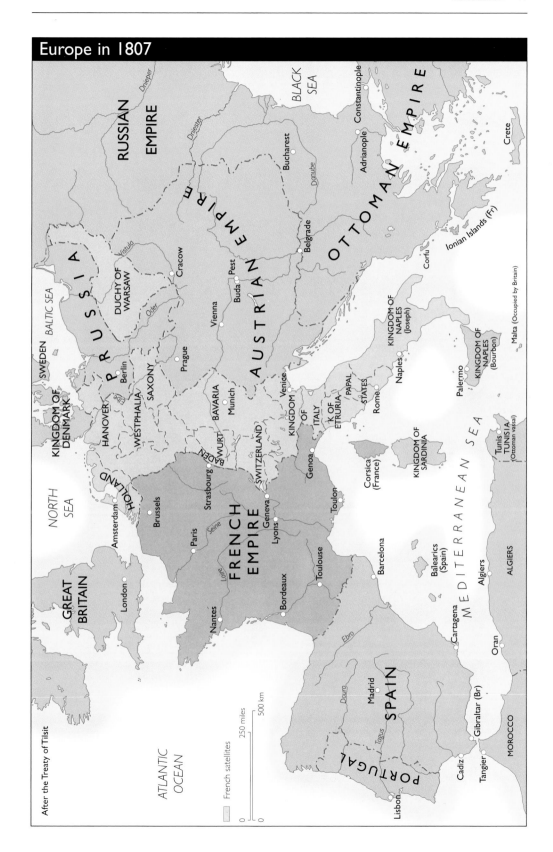

After the Treaty of Tilsit

French satellites

250 miles

500 km

ATLANTIC
OCEAN

GREAT
BRITAIN

London

NORTH
SEA

Amsterdam

HOLLAND

Brussels

Paris

Seine

Loire

Nantes

Bordeaux

Toulouse

FRENCH
EMPIRE

Strasbourg

Geneva

Lyons

SWITZERLAND

BADEN

WURT

BAVARIA

Munich

Toulon

Genoa

Corsica
(France)

KINGDOM
OF
ITALY

K OF
ETRURIA

PAPAL
STATES

Rome

Venice

Naples

KINGDOM OF
NAPLES
(Joseph)

KINGDOM OF
SARDINIA

Palermo

KINGDOM
OF
NAPLES
(Bourbon)

Malta (Occupied by Britain)

Tunis
TUNISIA
(Ottoman vassal)

MEDITERRANEAN SEA

Balearics
(Spain)

Barcelona

Algiers

ALGIERS

Cartagena

Oran

SPAIN

Madrid

Douro

Tagus

Ebro

PORTUGAL

Lisbon

Cadiz

Tangier

Gibraltar (Br)

MOROCCO

SWEDEN

BALTIC SEA

KINGDOM OF
DENMARK

HANOVER

WESTPHALIA

SAXONY

Berlin

P R U S S I A

Elbe

Oder

Vistula

DUCHY OF
WARSAW

Cracow

Prague

Vienna

Buda   Pest

A U S T R I A N

E M P I R E

RUSSIAN
EMPIRE

Dnieper

Dniester

Danube

Bucharest

Belgrade

BLACK
SEA

Constantinople

Adrianople

OTTOMAN   EMPIRE

Corfu

Ionian Islands (Fr)

Crete

Chronology

1807 **18 October** French troops cross into Spain *en route* to Portugal.
27 October France and Spain conclude the Treaty of Fontainebleau.
30 November Junot occupies Lisbon.

1808 **16 February** French troops enter Spain.
17 March King Charles IV of Spain abdicates.
23 March French troops occupy Madrid.
16 April Conference at Bayonne opens.
2 May *Dos de Mayo*: Madrid uprising; Murat quells it with great ferocity.
6 June Joseph Bonaparte proclaimed King of Spain.
8 June Asturian junta appeals for aid from Britain.
15 June–13 August First siege of Saragossa.
14 July Bessières defeats the Spanish under Cuesta, and under Blake at Medina del Rio Seco.
21 July General Dupont surrenders his corps at Bailen.
1 August Wellesley's army lands at Mondego Bay, Portugal; Joseph evacuates Madrid.
17 August Wellesley defeats the French at Roliça.
21 August Wellesley defeats Junot at Vimiero.
30 August Convention of Cintra. French troops to be repatriated.
September Representatives of the provincial juntas form the Central Junta at Aranjuez.
30 October French evacuate Portugal.
4 November Napoleon arrives in Spain at the head of 125,000 troops to attack the Spanish armies on the line of the Ebro.
10 November Battles of Espinosa and Gamonal.
23 November Battle of Tudela. French defeat the Spanish.
29–30 November Battle of Somosierra.

4 December Napoleon enters Madrid.
10 December Sir John Moore advances from Salamanca.
20 December Second siege of Saragossa begins.
25 December–14 January Retreat to Corunna.

1809 **13 January** Victor defeats Venegas at Ucles.
16 January Battle of Corunna. Moore, though victorious, is killed. His army safely disembarks two days later.
20 February Fall of Saragossa after a dreadful three-month siege in which approximately 50,000 people perish.
22 March French take Oporto. Central Junta proposes a new reformed Cortes.
28 March Battle of Medellin. Victor defeats Cuesta.
22 April Wellesley arrives back in Portugal.
12 May Wellesley, having crossed the Douro, defeats Soult at Oporto.
24 May Siege of Gerona begins.
27–28 July Wellesley defeats the French at Talavera.
18 October Spanish victory at Tamames.
20 October Construction of the Lines of Torres Vedras begins.
19 November Mortier defeats the Spanish at Ocaña and Alba de Tormes.
11 December Fall of Gerona.

1810 **January** French conquer Andalusia. A coup ousts the Central Junta.
5 February French troops invest Cadiz, seat of the new regency, which lasts two years.
April–May Various juntas in Spanish America declare independence.
10 July Masséna captures Ciudad Rodrigo.
24 July Ney defeats Craufurd at the River Coa.
28 July Almeida surrenders.
16 September Revolt in Mexico.
24 September The new Cortes convenes near Cadiz and soon moves there.

27 September Battle of Busaco. Wellington defeats Masséna.

10 October Wellesley occupies a defensive position behind the Lines of Torres Vedras.

14 October Masséna encounters the Lines and halts.

16 November French troops retreat from the Lines of Torres Vedras.

1811
26 January French lay siege to Badajoz.

19 February Soult defeats the Spanish at the Gebora River.

5 March Graham victorious at Barrosa; French leave Portugal.

9 March Badajoz falls to the French.

15 March Masséna withdraws to Spain.

3–5 May Battle of Fuentes de Oñoro. Wellington defeats Masséna.

6–15 May First British siege of Badajoz.

1 May Wellington occupies Almeida.

16 May Battle of Albuera. Beresford defeats Soult but is badly mauled in the process.

19 May–17 June Second British siege of Badajoz. They fail.

5 July Venezuela declares independence from Spain.

25 September Battle of El Bodon.

1812
8 January Opening of the siege of Ciudad Rodrigo.

19 January British storm and capture Ciudad Rodrigo.

16 March Wellington begins the third siege of Badajoz.

19 March The Cortes issues the liberal constitution of Cadiz, which guarantees freedom of the press, but not of religion, together with a legal code to apply throughout the country.

6–7 April Wellington takes Badajoz by storm.

22 July Battle of Salamanca. Marmont decisively defeated.

12 August Wellington enters Madrid.

24 August French abandon siege of Cadiz.

19 September–22 October Wellington besieges Burgos, but fails to take it.

2 October Wellington appointed C-in-C of the Spanish armies.

22 October–19 November Allies retreat from Burgos to Ciudad Rodrigo, abandoning Madrid on 30 October.

2 November French reoccupy Madrid.

1813
22 May Wellington opens his offensive.

27 May French evacuate Madrid.

2 June Allies besiege Tarragona.

3 June Allies cross the Douro.

13 June French abandon Burgos; Allies abandon siege of Tarragona.

17 June Wellington crosses the Ebro.

21 June Battle of Vitoria. Wellington decisively defeats King Joseph.

28 June Siege of San Sebastian begins.

30 June Siege of Pamplona begins.

11 July Soult takes command of French troops at the Pyrenees.

25 July Soult counterattacks in the Pyrenees at Maya and Roncesvalles.

28–30 July Wellington defeats Soult at Sorauren.

31 August Graham captures San Sebastian; Battle of Vera; Wellington repulses Soult at San Marcial.

8 September Citadel at San Sebastian capitulates.

7 October Allied troops cross the Bidassoa and enter French territory.

31 October French surrender Pamplona.

10 November Wellington defeats Soult at the River Nivelle.

9–12 December Wellington defeats Soult at the River Nive.

11 December Treaty of Valençay. Napoleon releases King Ferdinand from captivity in exchange for Ferdinand's (unfulfilled) promise of peace.

13 December Action at St. Pierre. Hill repulses Soult; Ferdinand restored to the Spanish throne.

1814
26 February Allies besiege Bayonne.

27 February Wellington defeats Soult at Orthez.

20 March Action at Tarbes.

24 March Ferdinand VII returns to Spain.

6 April Napoleon abdicates unconditionally in Paris.

10 April Wellington defeats Soult at Toulouse.

14 April French sortie from Bayonne.

17 April Soult surrenders.

27 April Bayonne surrenders.

30 April Treaty of Paris.

Perennial foes: Britain, France and Spain

The centuries that preceded the Peninsular War were marked by regular periods of confrontation between Britain, France, and Spain in a series of constantly shifting alliances and loyalties. Anglo-French hostility, however, was consistent. These powers were known as 'hereditary' enemies by contemporaries with good reason. The table below summarizes the conflicts waged in the century before the Peninsular War between Europe's three oldest unified nations.

Up to 1792, these conflicts were, of course, those of kings, and followed the pattern of eighteenth-century warfare: sovereigns sought limited objectives and entertained no desire to overthrow their adversaries' ruling (and indeed usually ancient) dynasty. The outbreak of the French Revolution in 1789 altered this pattern forever and international relations underwent some radical changes as a result.

In the realm of power politics the eighteenth century was a period of nearly continuous rivalry between France and Britain, fueled by colonial and commercial rivalry, and heightened by the basic tenet of British foreign policy that the Continent remain free from a single hegemonic power. In short, Britain would not tolerate an imbalance of power that furnished an overwhelming advantage to any of the other Great Powers – France, Austria, Russia, and Prussia. As France had consistently sought to upset this balance, most particularly since the accession of Louis XIV, Anglo-French hostility was a natural and frequent product of Bourbon French ambitions.

Many British contemporaries held that the changing nature of international relations brought about by the French Revolution would eliminate the grounds of suspicion between these traditional rivals. Yet on the contrary, they became fiercer opponents than ever, more strongly opposed by the introduction of radically different political ideologies, now fused with the same old colonial and commercial disputes and, above all, with the French revolutionaries' desire for territorial expansion. All this was a much more potent mix than had been the traditional ingredients of Anglo-French enmity. The occupation of the Low Countries

---

Conflicts between Britain, Spain, and France 1702–1808

1702–1714	Britain vs. France and Spain	War of the Spanish Succession
1718–20	Britain and France vs. Spain	War of the Quadruple Alliance
1739–48	Britain vs. Spain	War of Jenkins's Ear
1740–48	Britain vs. France	War of the Austrian Succession
1756–63	Britain vs. France	Seven Years' War
1778–83	Britain vs. France	War of American Independence
1779–93	Britain vs. Spain	War of American Independence
1793–1802	Britain vs. France	French Revolutionary Wars
1793–95	Spain vs. France	French Revolutionary Wars
1796–1802	Britain vs. Spain	French Revolutionary Wars
1803–14/15	Britain vs. France	Napoleonic Wars
1804–1808	Britain vs. Spain	Napoleonic Wars

Death of General Wolfe at Quebec, 13 September 1759. Anglo-French rivalry in the eighteenth century involved hostilities throughout the world, particularly in North America, where French Canada and Britain's 13 colonies provided a fertile killing ground. When the Seven Years' War ended in 1763, having been waged in Europe, North America, India, and across the oceans of the world, Britain emerged supreme, annexing Canada and parts of India from France. (Ann Ronan Picture Library)

during the French Revolutionary Wars posed, for instance, an insuperable barrier to good relations between the two countries. In short, Britain considered any power with a strong navy which controlled the Low Countries to be a threat to her very existence.

After nearly a decade of conflict between 1793 and 1802, Britain and France concluded a very tenuous peace at Amiens, but Napoleon's continued incursions into Switzerland, Holland, Germany, and Italy, and Britain's refusal to evacuate Malta as protection against French expansion in the Mediterranean meant that the renewal of hostilities in May 1803 was inevitable. This opening phase of the Napoleonic Wars, confined until the summer of 1805 to Britain and France, was by the nature of their respective armed forces largely restricted to naval activity. The Peninsular War changed this dramatically by offering Britain the opportunity to confront France on the soil of a friendly power, easily accessible by sea.

Yet relations between Spain and Britain had, historically, been far from amicable. In

1790 Britain and Spain nearly went to war over the Nootka Sound crisis, a territorial dispute concerning the coast of present-day British Columbia. France and Spain had an alliance, but the National Assembly refused to honor a treaty signed prior to the Revolution. The feeble position of Louis XVI, still king but with restricted powers, attracted the sympathy of the Spanish ruling house which was Bourbon, like that of Louis. Yet the Revolution meant that the French and Spanish sovereigns could no longer rely on the 'Family Compact' established between them. Increasing humiliations perpetrated against Louis, and the steady stream of French emigrés crossing the Pyrenees, inevitably turned Spain against the revolutionaries. Spain offered sanctuary to the French royal family but the revolutionaries twice refused to allow this before finally declaring war on Spain on 7 March 1793.

Spain enjoyed initial success in the campaign that followed. One army defended the western Pyrenees against all French incursions, while another invaded Roussillon and western Provence. However, Spanish conduct at the siege of Toulon at the close of the year was disgraceful, and in 1794 Spain's two best commanders died. Later that year the French counterattacked with superior strength, taking the border fortresses and penetrating nearly to the line of the River Ebro. Military reverses and economic dislocation led Spain formally to withdraw from the war by concluding the Treaty of Basle on 22 July 1795. She ceded Santo Domingo (the present-day Dominican Republic) to France in exchange for French withdrawal from Spanish territory.

In the following year, 1796, the Treaty of San Ildefonso allied Spain to France, against Britain. As this required Spain to furnish

British surrender at Yorktown, 1781. The War of
American Independence (1775–1783) offered France
the opportunity to avenge her losses in the Seven Years'
and the French and Indian War (1756–1763) by assisting
the rebellious American colonists. Indeed, French military,
naval, and financial aid proved decisive, particularly at
Yorktown, where General Cornwallis surrendered
7,000 troops not merely to American, but to thousands
of French troops, who had isolated the British army
on the Virginia coast with the vital support of a French
fleet under de Grasse. (Ann Ronan Picture Library)

25 ships to the war effort, the stage was
set for a period of worldwide naval
confrontation between Spain and Britain
which lasted from 1796 until the Peace of
Amiens in 1802.

Spanish ties with France were
strengthened when on 7 October 1800 the
two countries signed the Convention of San
Ildefonso, which was later confirmed by the
Treaty of Aranjuez on 21 March 1801. British
interests were further damaged when, by the
Treaty of Badajoz with France, Spain agreed
to wage war against Britain's long-standing
ally, Portugal. The so-called 'War of the
Oranges' was short (May and June 1801) but
by the peace signed on 6 June Spain annexed
the small frontier district of Olivenza and

Portugal was forced to close its ports to
British ships and to pay France a reparation
of 20 million francs.

During the period of Anglo-Spanish
hostilities from 1796 to 1802, operations were
almost exclusively naval. On paper, at least,
Spain appeared a formidable opponent. In
1793 the Spanish Empire stretched over vast
reaches of the Americas, including a million
square miles (2.6 million square kilometers)
west of the Mississippi, and extended to
possessions in the Caribbean (chiefly Cuba)
and in the Pacific (chiefly the Philippines).
She was the third ranked naval power in the
world, with 76 ships-of-the-line (of which
56 were actually in commission) and
105 smaller vessels.

Nevertheless, the Spanish navy proved no
match for the Royal Navy. In practically every
encounter, from cutting-out operations to
ship-to-ship actions to fleet engagements, the
Spanish were defeated, both in home and in
colonial waters. Notable exceptions included
an unsuccessful British attack against San
Juan, Puerto Rico in 1797 and Nelson's foray
against Santa Cruz de Tenerife in the Canary
Islands in the same year. Nevertheless, the

Battle of Cape St Vincent, fought in February 1797, was a notable British triumph. Indeed, the defeat suffered at St Vincent was enough to force the Spanish fleet back to Cadiz for the remainder of the war, and notwithstanding Nelson's bloody repulse at Tenerife, the Spanish fleet had been effectively neutralized. This situation not only adversely affected Spain's trade with, and administration of, her overseas colonies, it halted ship building altogether: Spain launched its last ship-of-the-line in 1798 and the last frigate two years later. To crown the country's misfortunes, British troops easily captured Minorca in 1798.

Although the Treaty of Amiens brought peace, albeit short-lived, between Britain and Spain in March 1802, the Anglo-French contest resumed only 14 months later, and it was not long before Spain was once again drawn into the conflict. On 9 October 1803 France effectively coerced Spain into an alliance which required her to supply a monthly payment of 6 million francs, to enforce Portuguese neutrality and to provide France with between 25 and 29 ships-of-the-line. Napoleon intended to use these to protect his cross-Channel invasion force.

Nevertheless, this agreement did not oblige Spain to enter hostilities against Britain and therefore its existence was as yet unknown by the Admiralty in London. Yet as the months passed Spain's repeated claims of neutrality in the Anglo-French conflict rang increasingly hollow and it became impossible for Britain to tolerate what amounted to Spain's funding of Napoleon's war against her: confrontation with Spain was only a matter of time. The approach off Cadiz of a fleet carrying treasure from Peru precipitated it, and, without a previous declaration of war a Royal Navy squadron attacked on 5 October 1804. Outraged, Spain formally declared war on 12 December, thus providing Napoleon with the opportunity he had long hoped for to make use of the sizable, though decrepit, Spanish fleet. By combining it with his own he hoped to draw the Channel fleet out to sea and thus provide the short interval needed to thrust his army of invasion, which was camped at Boulogne on the north coast of France, across that narrow stretch of water which for centuries had protected his rivals. As is well known, Vice-Admiral Horatio Nelson (1758--1805) shattered Napoleon's plans at Trafalgar on 21 October 1805, when the Franco-Spanish fleet was virtually annihilated in one of the greatest contests in the history of naval warfare.

This did not, however, spell the end of Anglo-Spanish hostility, and in the following year a British expedition to Spanish America captured Buenos Aires and Montevideo (in present-day Argentina and Uruguay, respectively). Both cities fell to British troops, but the garrisons quickly found themselves confronted by overwhelming numbers of colonial militia and Spanish regulars and were forced to surrender. A relieving force arrived in January 1807 and retook Montevideo, but it was defeated at Buenos Aires and all British troops were withdrawn the following month. Thus, in 1807, on the eve of the Peninsular War, Britain and Spain remained at war. Quite how the relationship between Britain and Spain could have undergone such a radical shift in the course of a single year will be covered later.

Opposing forces

The British Army

Throughout the eighteenth century and into the Napoleonic Wars Britain remained a largely self-reliant nation whose strength derived mainly from the Royal Navy, unquestionably the greatest maritime force of its day. Geography and superior naval power had meant that only a small standing army was necessary for the country's defense. In any event the size of the army was limited by financial and above all political considerations. A mistrust of the military amongst Parliament and nation was a legacy dating back to the Commonwealth, under

Lieutenant-General Sir John Moore (1761–1809). Adored by his men, Moore was instrumental in improving light infantry training before becoming C-in-C of the British Army in the Peninsula in 1808. While advancing into Spain to confront overwhelming French forces he found himself badly unsupported by the Spanish and forced to make a disastrous retreat to Corunna, where he was killed. His victory there, however, ensured the army's safe evacuation. (Ann Ronan Picture Library)

Cromwell, who had used the army as an instrument of despotism. Suspicion continued under the Restoration, making the army feared and in some cases even despised as the enemy of liberty. The regular army lived on the margins of society, supplying garrisons for the colonies and Ireland. New units were raised on the outbreak of war and disbanded at the peace. Home defense was the responsibility of the Navy as the first line of defense and the Militia as the second.

Recruiting methods and the social make-up of the British Army remained effectively unchanged from its eighteenth-century forebears, such that the professional and mercantile classes scarcely appeared in the officer corps, making the army highly divided on class lines. The officer corps was the preserve of the aristocracy (mostly confined to the Guards and cavalry) and, above all, the gentry. This situation was perpetuated by the purchase system: gentlemen aspiring to an officer's rank had to possess sufficient funds to buy their regimental commissions. The monopoly of wealth and social connection all but guaranteed that the upper ranks remained in the hands of the ruling classes. In this respect it bore no relation to its French counterpart. The reforms of the Revolution had swept away such forms of privilege and it was said that every soldier carried a marshal's baton in his knapsack – an allusion to meritocratic promotion.

British officers were generally brave and possessed a social status that commanded respect and obedience from the men under their leadership. Officers were expected to lead from the front, with predictably high rates of casualties. The ordinary ranks were, unlike the French, volunteers, drawn to the colors by bounty and, being the poorest elements of society, shared nothing in

Sir Arthur Wellesley, 1st Duke of Wellington (1769–1852). Born into an aristocratic Anglo-Irish family, Wellington remains the greatest of many exceptionally skilled commanders produced by the British Army, including the accomplished Marlborough. Highly intelligent and hard-working, Wellington first distinguished himself in India before leading Anglo-Portuguese and, later, Spanish forces in the Peninsula. He conceived the brilliant defenses of Torres Vedras and though he was not adept at siege warfare he won every battle in which he was present. (Oil by Sir T. Lawrence, Edimedia)

wished to escape from poverty or to seek adventure. Whatever their background, over time Wellington molded them into a first-rate fighting force and he was impressed by the change wrought in his men by army life: 'It is really wonderful,' he wrote during the war, 'that we should have made them the fine fellows they are.'

The British Army had its reformers in men such as Sir Ralph Abercromby (1734–1801) and Sir John Moore (1761–1809), but no personality put a greater stamp on this period than Wellington. Wellington embodied eighteenth-century stability, and

common with their officers. Indeed, the only link between them were the sergeants and other non-commissioned officers.

Although officially a volunteer force, the British Army certainly contained an element of unwilling recruits: criminals and vagabonds, thugs and ruffians who were only serving to avoid a prison sentence. It is however important to rectify a common misconception on this subject: when Wellington wrote of 'the scum of the earth,' he was referring not to the army in general, but to that element which plundered in the wake of the Battle of Vitoria. It is probably fair to say that most ordinary soldiers simply

Wellington and his generals, 1813. Remarkably little in the Duke's performance in the Peninsula can be criticized, apart from his failure to provide his subordinates with opportunities for independent command. As C-in-C he refused to appoint a second-in-command and until the very end of the war he rarely delegated authority over the troops except at divisional level – possibly the consequence of Beresford's near disaster at Albuera. (After Heaphy, National Army Museum)

Major-General Sir Edward Pakenham (1778–1815). Wellington's brother-in-law, Pakenham took a prominent part in the victory at Salamanca, where he assaulted the head of the French column of march. The C-in-C said of him afterwards: 'Pakenham may not be the brightest genius, but my partiality for him does not lead me astray, when I tell you he is one of the best we have.' He was killed at New Orleans in 1815 during the war against the United States. (National Army Museum)

did not undertake any fundamental change to a system which appeared to function well.

However it is easy in hindsight to assume that when the British Army landed in Portugal in 1808 victory was only a matter of time. This was by no means the case, and the record of the army since 1793 was not a wholly unblemished one. Apart from the campaigns in Egypt in 1801, and Copenhagen in 1807, many of the expeditions had achieved only limited success, or, such as at Buenos Aires and Rosetta as recently as 1807, were outright failures. The reputation so tarnished in the War of American Independence had yet to be fully restored, despite the reforms and inspiration of such men as Abercromby and Moore.

Nevertheless, Wellington maximized the effectiveness of the system he inherited. As Commander-in-Chief in the Peninsula, Wellington chose to have a tiny staff headquarters and no second-in-command, keeping matters in his own hands and those of a few key officers, particularly the

Quartermaster-General, the Adjutant-General, the head of the Commissariat, the Chief of Artillery, and the Chief Engineer. He relied heavily on his intelligence network, acquiring useful information on French strength, plans and dispositions from his own superb intelligence officers, 'correspondents', and observers throughout the Peninsula, and from civilians and guerrillas, who provided much useful information through simple observation or by interdicting French dispatches.

Wellington took great pains to see that the Commissariat kept his army well supplied with the necessities of war: food, clothing, and ammunition. In this he held a significant advantage over the French army, which suffered a chronic shortage of all matériel and could not feed itself without recourse to plunder. The Peninsula lacked the fertile plains of Germany and Italy, but Wellington could compensate by using unrestricted access to the sea to obtain supplies and, however poor the inhabitants of Iberia, at least they were friendly. He developed an effective system of depots which provided for the needs of tens of thousands of men and animals, both horses and the livestock which supplied meat for the army.

The result of Wellington's personal attention to the administration, supply and training of the army was the creation of one of the greatest fighting forces of modern times. As he himself claimed in 1813: 'It is probably the most complete machine for its number now existing in Europe.' Their record on the battlefield is a worthy testament to Wellington's achievement, for they never lost a battle. Their commander proudly acknowledged: 'I have the satisfaction of reflecting that, having tried them frequently, they have never failed me.'

The French Army

The French armies in the Peninsula in the early years of the war were large, but most of the men were raw recruits, about one third drawn early from the levies of 1808 and 1809. They also contained soldiers of many

Joseph Bonaparte (1768–1844), King of Spain. In 1808 Napoleon's eldest brother reluctantly left the throne of Naples in exchange for that of the Empire's most recent conquest. He lacked popular support in a country he could never wholly subdue, received constant criticism and interference from Napoleon, and held no authority over French generals in the field. As a result, Joseph repeatedly sought to abdicate – a wish the Emperor did not grant until after the disaster at Vitoria in 1813. (Ann Ronan Picture Library)

needs, with many people already living at subsistence levels, the French found their freedom of movement severely impaired and relied ever more strongly on plunder and requisitions of the civilian population. As there was no overall commander in the Peninsula there was often no coordination between the various armies, which were scattered across Spain and struggled to maintain communications along its primitive and often nonexistent roads.

French generals were shameless in stripping the assets of the towns they occupied, stealing art and raiding treasuries as they went. It is not surprising that French soldiers in their disillusionment would decry their leaders' avarice while they themselves struggled just to keep themselves fed. 'This war in Spain,' ran the popular sentiment of the ordinary ranks, 'means death for the men, ruin for the officers, a fortune for the generals.'

nationalities, many of whose countries had been absorbed into the Empire. Poles, Swiss, Germans from the states of the Confederation of the Rhine, volunteer Irish, Italians, and Neapolitans, all served in the Peninsula, with different degrees of willingness and skill. Over 50,000 Italians alone fought as French allies. Many of the Germans deserted when opportunity presented itself, joining the King's German Legion, a fine corps of Hanoverians formed in 1803 during the French occupation of this north German patrimony of George III.

The French employed those tactics that they had used with such consistent success in the past on the battlefields of western and central Europe: concentration of artillery and massed attack in column. Their armies were accustomed to 'living off the land,' and as such did not establish the network of supply depots which Wellington wisely did. As the land was found woefully deficient for their

Marshal André Masséna (1758–1817). Though distinguished in numerous campaigns since the 1790s, he was far less successful in the Peninsula. Defeated at Busaco in 1810, Masséna failed to penetrate the Lines of Torres Vedras and was beaten again at Fuentes de Oñoro in 1811, before being recalled. Wellington nevertheless considered him a worthy opponent: 'When Masséna was opposed to me I could not eat, drink or sleep. I never knew what repose or respite from anxiety was. I was kept perpetually on the alert.' (Ann Ronan Picture Library)

Marshal Nicolas Soult (1769–1851). Commander during the later stages of the pursuit of Moore to Corunna, Soult was later defeated at Oporto in 1809 and ejected from Portugal. Although he subsequently enjoyed great success against the Spanish at Ocaña and elsewhere, he performed badly at Albuera in 1811. Recalled for service in Germany in 1813, he returned to Spain after the Battle of Vitoria and was appointed C-in-C, in which capacity he demonstrated considerable skill in opposing Wellington's advance. (Ann Ronan Picture Library)

The Spanish Army

In 1808 the army stood at slightly over 100,000 men and about 30,000 troops mobilized from the militia. Spain's regular forces were amongst the worst in Europe at the start of the Peninsular War, but by the end of the conflict had improved on their appalling record. Administered by corrupt and incompetent officials, the infantry was severely lacking in officers, who themselves received virtually no training. Surtees, a soldier in the 95th Rifles, called them 'the most contemptible creatures that I ever beheld … utterly unfit and unable to command their men.' Leith Hay, another British soldier, described the army as '… ill-commanded, ill-appointed, moderately disciplined and in most respects inefficient …' Units were composed of volunteers and of conscripts, who came from the lowest classes. Promotion was all but impossible in a system where rising through the ranks effectively ceased at the rank of captain. Higher ranks were held by aristocrats and landowners who had neither knowledge of nor interest in soldiering. Not only were the officers deficient in training or motivation, the army authorized no official drill, leaving every unit commander to devise his own field instructions as he saw fit. Unit effectiveness was further undermined by insufficient numbers, equipment and food, and the cavalry suffered from an acute shortage of mounts, with fewer than one third of its troopers supplied with a horse.

The most respectable units of the Spanish army were those of the Marquis de la Romana, whose division had been sent to north Germany to serve with Napoleon's troops. On hearing of the uprising in Madrid, Romana's men revolted, were evacuated by the Royal Navy, and returned for service in Spain. Even these relatively well-led and well-equipped troops were described by one British soldier as having '… more the appearance of a large body of peasants … in want of everything, than a regular army.' During the retreat to Corunna Surtees found them '… [even] in their best days, more like an armed mob than regularly organized soldiers.'

If the soldiers were bad, the commanders were beyond contempt. With few exceptions they were a liability in the field, not merely to their own troops but to the British as well. They provided erroneous information to Moore, which led to the disastrous retreat to Corunna, they failed either to support or to supply Wellington after Talavera, and they were widely known for their corrupt practices. Eventually Wellington took personal command of the Spanish armies, and only then was he able to rely upon them.

The cavalry consistently performed so badly that any success was seen with astonishment. The infantry was prone to panic and flee, casting away their weapons in the stampede for the rear. Contempt for such men in the British ranks was not surprising, though it must be remembered that low morale was the natural result of poor leadership, irregular pay and food, and a chronic lack of equipment and clothing.

When properly led and supplied the Spanish could perform well, as at Vitoria and in the Pyrenees and toward the close of the war standards had improved sufficiently to allow a small number of Spaniards to join the ranks of British regiments.

If the regular forces were abysmal, the civilian defenders of cities like Saragossa and Gerona were an entirely different breed, demonstrating immense courage in the face of French troops and heroic feats of resistance and hardship under siege. The Church and landowners supported all such forms of resistance as well as the guerrillas,

who were infamous for their cruelty. The French retaliated in kind with revenge on a grand scale. These will be described elsewhere.

The Portuguese Army

General Andoche Junot (1771–1813) disbanded the Portuguese army during his occupation of the country and it was not resurrected until Wellington assigned General William Beresford (1764–1854) the task of raising and organizing new units which were then incorporated into British brigades. Like the Spanish, the Portuguese officers were badly paid and had no opportunity for advancement. A man could remain a captain for literally decades. William Warre, a Portuguese-born British officer, noted in 1808 that the Portuguese were '... cowards who won't fight a

Spanish guerrillas. As shown, guerrillas were variously armed and clothed, depending on the availability of Spanish, British or captured French weapons and uniforms and the particular tastes of the partisans themselves. The figure on the left is dressed entirely in civilian clothes and carries an antiquated blunderbuss, while the other two men wear vestiges of military dress, particularly the cavalryman on the right. (Roger-Viollet)

one-sixteenth of a Frenchman with arms, but plunder and murder the wounded ...' The following year he found the men '... well enough, very obedient, willing, and patient, but also naturally dirty and careless of their persons ... The Officers ... are detestable, mean, ignorant ...'

Beresford found the army numbering half its establishment, with only 30,000 instead of nearly 60,000. This was changed through conscription, while Beresford instituted wide-ranging and effective reforms, including the retirement of inefficient and indolent officers, and the addition of British officers to the regiments and higher command structure. These men were so positioned as to have Portuguese officers above and below them; likewise, all Portuguese officers had British superiors and subordinates. A Portuguese regiment might therefore have a British colonel, but below him Portuguese majors. Non-commissioned officers and men received better pay, training, food, and equipment, which in turn raised morale and produced improved results on the battlefield. Warre remarked in the spring of 1809 that, 'The Portuguese immediately under the instruction of British officers are coming on very well ... The men may be made anything we please of, with proper management ...' Others noted over time that the Portuguese bore the fatigues and privations of campaigning without complaint and showed considerable bravery in action.

By 1812 a number of British observers commented that the Portuguese were fine soldiers and in some cases fought on a par with their British counterparts, and Wellington would call them 'the fighting cocks of the army.' As early as at Busaco in 1810 Schaumann remarked how 'The Portuguese fought with conspicuous courage ... They behaved just like English troops.' Apart from the regular soldiers there were the mule-drivers and camp-followers, who gained a dreadful reputation for pillaging and the murder of French wounded after battle. Unlike the infantry, the Portuguese cavalry and siege train never improved. A shortage of horses plagued the former and obsolete equipment the latter.

The Portuguese contribution to the war was important, and while it is natural to think of Wellington's army as 'British', it is only right to observe that by 1810 it was nearly half Portuguese. Beresford performed his task well, and his soldiers made a solid contribution to the Allied victory.

Origins of the conflict

June 1807 marked the high water mark of Napoleonic fortunes. On the 14th Napoleon routed the Russian army at Friedland and on the 25th he and Tsar Alexander met on a raft in the Niemen River at Tilsit to make peace. Not only did Russia conclude peace (together with Prussia), she went so far as to form an alliance with France against Britain, thus leaving Napoleon supreme in Europe. He had cowed the three great continental powers, Austria, Prussia and Russia, in three successive and brilliant campaigns, and only Britain, Sweden, and Portugal remained to oppose him. Trafalgar, fought two years before, had not only saved Britain from imminent invasion, it had established her as mistress of the seas, leaving France no means of striking at her most implacable foe except by severing her trade links with the Continent. This Napoleon duly attempted when, immediately after subduing Prussia in 1806, he issued the Berlin Decrees, which banned British and British colonial goods from all territory under French control. This was the beginning of his 'Continental System', a novel attempt first to isolate and then to starve Britain into submission. Britain instituted a novel reply: rather than eliminate French trade through blockade, she sought to regulate it. Vessels flying the tricolor or those of the French satellites were fair game for British warships; those of neutral countries wishing to trade with France could only do so under heavy restrictions.

British maritime policy was to have serious implications for Anglo-American relations and ultimately led to war between the countries in 1812. As British and British colonial goods were in great demand on the Continent, Napoleon's system became increasingly unpopular throughout the Empire – and even in France herself – making smuggling rampant along practically

every coast. This, in turn, drove Napoleon to tighten and, above all, expand his control over the few remaining territories not yet subject to his rule. He had little trouble conquering southern Italy in 1806, but this left neutral Portugal as the last country still defying his plan. Control of Portugal meant control of her colonial trade, above all with Brazil. Access to Spain's colonies was even more coveted, encompassing as they did most of South and Central America.

The opportunity to plug this gap in the Continental System came after Tilsit, when Napoleon and Alexander agreed to cooperate in the closure of continental ports to British trade. This agreement extended as far west as Portugal, and here may be found the origins of the Peninsular War. With the sole exception of Portugal, France already controlled the European coastline from the Niemen to the Adriatic, and thus Napoleon relied on his Spanish ally to allow the passage of French troops across the Pyrenees. Only in this way could he compel Portugal to adopt the Continental System.

Long at odds with her more powerful neighbor, Spain, Portugal, with her extensive Atlantic coastline, had since the Middle Ages depended on maritime trade with Britain, which by 1807 accounted for almost half that trade. Over the centuries Portugal had remained steadfastly linked to Britain, and had defied French attempts to coerce her cooperation. Portugal had remained neutral since the start of the conflict in 1803, but she had irritated the French emperor by permitting ships of the Royal Navy to use the Tagus estuary as a base for shelter and provisioning. This, in combination with her total defiance of the Continental System, rendered Portugal a natural target for French occupation, not least because Tilsit had put an end to fighting elsewhere, releasing

Principal battles and sieges

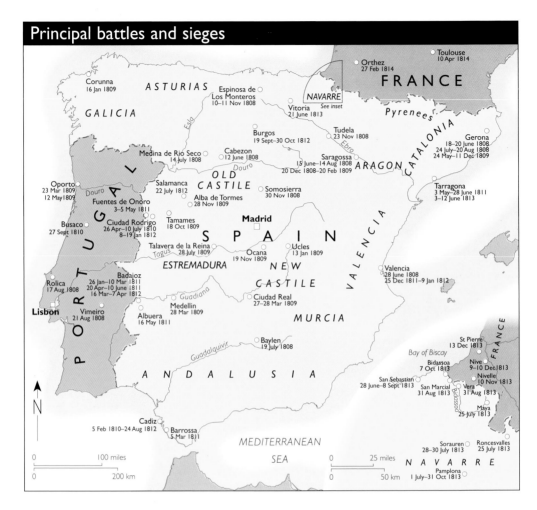

Every province in Spain and Portugal experienced fighting in one form or another, ranging from minor skirmishes between companies or battalions to major battles and sieges, involving tens of thousands of combatants on both sides. Most of the principal actions fought in the Peninsular War are shown here. In contrast to many other Napoleonic theaters of war, the Peninsula witnessed numerous major – and often extremely bitter – sieges, some conducted between Anglo-Portuguese and French forces, others solely between the French and Spanish. Some of the main sieges included: Cadiz, Valencia, Gerona, San Sebastian, Saragossa, Tarragona, Burgos, Badajoz, and Ciudad Rodrigo. The last two were of particular strategic importance, being the key points of passage between Portugal and Spain.

French forces for operations against a weak country which also shared a long frontier with an ally of France.

Portugal was ruled by the Prince Regent, John (1767–1826), of the House of Braganza.

His parents, King Peter III and Queen Maria I, had succeeded to the Portuguese throne as joint rulers in February 1777, but the King died in 1786. From 1792 onward their son acted as regent for the Queen, who had gone insane and remained so at the time of the French invasion. Tilsit had no sooner been signed than John received a series of threats and ultimata demanding adherence to French demands for the closure of Portuguese ports to British ships, commercial as well as naval. John had no wish to comply and made several futile attempts to placate the French with a series of concessions. Napoleon remained firm and orders were issued to Junot to cross the Pyrenees and invade Portugal. Needless to say, this required the cooperation of Spain, which had been obtained in the Treaty of

Fontainebleau, concluded on 27 October, and authorizing the passage of French troops across Spanish territory.

The subjugation of Portugal quickly followed. Spain duly granted permission for French troops to pass through the country, and on 17 October, 10 days before the agreement at Fontainebleau, Junot advanced with 24,000 men across the Pyrenees. On 19 November they passed through Alcantara into Portuguese territory. The Portuguese could offer only feeble resistance, but the march over appalling roads and horrendous terrain took a heavy toll on the invaders. When, at last, Junot entered Lisbon unopposed on 30 November, he did so with little more than 2,000 bedraggled men, the remainder strung out along the primitive roads. It was a hollow victory. The previous day the Regent, the royal family and its vast suite had abandoned the capital and taken refuge aboard a Royal Navy squadron in the harbor. They then departed for the Portuguese colony of Brazil, taking with them the Portuguese fleet and most of the state treasure.

If Napoleon did not, therefore, achieve all his objectives, he could be satisfied by the swift and practically bloodless conquest of Portugal, whose army Junot disbanded and whose territory Napoleon divided with Spain in accordance with Fontainebleau. He had achieved the closure of the Tagus to the Royal Navy and the termination of all trade between British and Portuguese home ports (although, of course, not those of the Portuguese empire).

The invasion of Portugal, as we have seen, had depended on Spanish cooperation, the inducement being the partition of the country. Yet the Treaty of Fontainebleau hid Napoleon's real intentions regarding Spain, with whom he was becoming increasingly frustrated. As noted earlier, Spain had fought revolutionary France from 1793 to 1795 when, after a poor performance on the Pyrenean front, she had withdrawn from the First Coalition and, in the following year, joined France against Britain until the conclusion of peace in 1802. In 1801 Spain had invaded Portugal and annexed territory.

Charles IV, King of Spain (1748–1819), and his family. His reign, which began in 1788, marked an end to the period of enlightenment under his father. Charles was a political nonentity who spent much of his time hunting and ignoring political matters large and small, thus allowing Prince Godoy and his half-mad queen, Maria Louisa, to bungle state affairs. After the conference at Bayonne Charles lived in exile in France and died in obscurity. (Goya, Prado Museum/Edimedia)

Yet apart from that gain her alliance with France had cost her the loss of Trinidad to Britain and the virtual destruction of her fleet. She was badly beaten at St Vincent in 1797 and then again at Trafalgar in 1805. Spanish policy thereafter was inconsistent: in February 1806 the First Minister, Godoy, made a proposal to Napoleon for the dismemberment of Portugal which came to nothing. After that Franco-Spanish relations began to sour, and when in the autumn Napoleon became embroiled in conflict with Prussia, which Godoy erroneously believed would win, Spain secretly planned to leave the unpopular French alliance.

Partly to ensure Spain's loyalty, Napoleon required the country to supply its best division, under the Marquis de la Romana, for service in Bernadotte's corps, which was then watching the Baltic coast. Spain was then rendered weaker, for the march to Portugal had provided Napoleon with an excuse to garrison key Spanish towns between Bayonne and the Portuguese border, in theory to secure the line of communications but in reality a cover for a full-scale occupation of Spain.

King Charles IV had assumed the Spanish throne on the death of his father in December

Manuel Godoy, Prince of Peace (1767–1851). Corrupt, immoral and an arch-schemer, Godoy became the lover of Queen Maria Louisa of Spain, and a close confidant of her idiot husband, King Charles IV. As First Minister Godoy concluded the Treaty of Basle, which ended the conflict with France in 1795. During the royal intrigues of 1807–1808 he backed the king against his son Ferdinand, thus encouraging French intervention in Spanish internal affairs. Here he is flushed out of hiding after the riots at Aranjuez in March 1808. (Ann Ronan Picture Library)

1788. Charles III, although a despot, had presided over a period of *Ilustracion* (enlightenment) during which the arts and sciences were encouraged and the economy thrived. In the two decades which followed until the Peninsular War Charles showed himself to be kind, though stupid and completely unfit to rule a major nation. His chief interest was hunting and he ruled Spain in nothing more than a nominal role, for he was strongly influenced by his wife, Maria Louisa of Parma. It was the Queen's favorite minister (and lover), Manuel de Godoy, who became chief minister in 1792 and held the reins of power. Godoy, dishonest and ineffective, had led the country into financial ruin, military incompetence and bureaucratic corruption. Over time he built up support within the court by carefully appointing his supporters and arresting or exiling those who opposed him. He grew rich through corruption and misappropriation of public funds. As chief minister it was Godoy who had persuaded Charles to sign the Treaty of Basle in 1795 which took Spain out of the war against France (hence his title 'Prince of Peace') and made the nations allies. The three leading political figures, the King and Godoy on the one hand, and the heir-apparent Crown Prince Ferdinand (1784–1833) on the other, hated one another. Each had the support of their own factions, creating a political vacuum which not only prevented any unified front against Napoleon, but gave the Emperor the opportunity to meddle in Spanish internal affairs.

Throughout the winter of 1807 French agents in Spain became increasingly involved in Spanish internal affairs, encouraging friction between the King and Godoy, and Ferdinand, all as a means of creating an atmosphere of chaos that the French could manipulate into requiring formal intervention on the pretext of mediating. Spain, under French control, would become a reliable partner within the empire, her long Atlantic and Mediterranean coastlines could be sealed against British trade, and the remainder of her fleet would be at French disposal. The Spanish political crisis

deepened when, on 29 October, Godoy persuaded the king to arrest Ferdinand, claiming that he was behind a plot to dethrone his father and murder his mother. Later, on 17 December, Napoleon issued the Milan Decree, reaffirming his other policies on the continental blockade and banning all British trade with the European mainland. Spain, as France's ally, officially supported the blockade, but in practice smuggling through her ports and extensive coastline was widespread and often ignored or even condoned by local or provincial officials. This did not go unnoticed in Paris.

Napoleon's plan was formally instituted on 16 February 1808 when he announced that, as Spain's ally, France was obliged to intervene to restore order in Spain's domestic affairs and would mediate between the rival political factions within the royal family. First, French troops were dispatched to occupy key points and fortresses in the northern provinces, including Pamplona, San Sebastian, Barcelona, and Figueras, to secure the passes through the Pyrenees; next Marshal Joachim Murat (1767–1815) proceeded into Spain with 118,000 troops, ostensibly to reinforce Junot in Portugal. They received a warm welcome as

they passed through the towns. Meanwhile, on 17 March, Charles, at Aranjuez, was confronted by a popular uprising against him and Godoy (the *Motin de Aranjuez*) led by the Royal Guards. This marked the first *pronunciamento*, or coup, carried out by soldiers in the country's history. With the encouragement of Ferdinand, a large mob sacked and burned Godoy's palace. Godoy, who barely escaped alive, was arrested, deposed, and forced into exile. The King's connection with Godoy made his position untenable and he abdicated on 20 March in favor of his son, who became Ferdinand VII.

A few days later, on 24 March, Murat entered Madrid. Charles had attempted to flee to Cadiz some days before but had been prevented from doing so by an angry mob. Continuing his ruse, Napoleon called the rival members of the royal family to Bayonne, just across the Franco-Spanish border, ostensibly for a conference of arbitration. Notwithstanding anti-French riots in Madrid on 1 April, Ferdinand left the capital on 10 April to meet Napoleon. The conference was convened on 5 May. In a matter of days Napoleon had forced both Charles and Ferdinand to abdicate their claims to the Spanish throne in favor of his own brother, Joseph (1768–1844), who, with the backing of pro-French elements in Spain, was created king on 6 June. Crowned on 7 July at Bayonne, he entered Madrid on the 20th. Charles meanwhile retired to Rome and Ferdinand was placed under house arrest in Valençay, where he would remain until 1814. Thus, as the Spanish Bourbons were interned, Joseph duly proceeded to Madrid to take up a throne whose illegitimacy was plain for all of Spain to see.

A war of contrasts

Operations in 1808

Napoleon's decision to overthrow Bourbon rule in Spain proved a great miscalculation. Open defiance against the treacherous occupation of the country, exacerbated by the attempts of French troops to escort the King's youngest son, Don Francisco, to France, led to an uprising in Madrid on 2 May 1808. Infuriated mobs of *Madrileños*, armed with knives, clubs, and makeshift weapons, slaughtered 130 French soldiers before Murat's cavalry ruthlessly cut them down in their hundreds in order to restore order. Reprisals followed the next day: those believed complicit in the revolt were shot outside the city. Meanwhile, Francophile

Popular uprising in Madrid, 2 May 1808. When rumors reached the capital of Ferdinand's deposition and a plan to remove the remainder of the Royal Family to captivity in France, the crowd gathered in the Puerta del Sol grew hostile and began to attack the French garrison. Violence rapidly spread throughout the city, to be finally quelled by Murat's cavalry. Here, the inhabitants, armed with muskets, blunderbusses and knives, confront a body of dragoons. (Lithograph by Raffet, Roger-Viollet)

elements were said to have called on Napoleon's brother Joseph to be 'elected' king. Infuriated by the imposition of a foreign monarch, Spaniards across the provinces raised the standard of revolt. Starting on 9 May at Oviedo, capital of the Asturias, they held Ferdinand up as a martyr to French political machinations and established *ad hoc* military forces through regional 'juntas', or legislative assemblies. These sprang up across the country at Oviedo (24 May), Saragossa (25 May), Galicia (30 May), Catalonia (7 June) and elsewhere. They appeared rapidly, but the juntas failed to coordinate their efforts or agree on a common objective except for the extirpation of the French from Spanish soil. The strength of feeling was great and the conflict would soon come to acquire a highly emotive charge distinctly its own, carrying the evocative name of *La Guerra de la Independencia* (the War of Independence). Within a few weeks entire armies sprang up. In Andalusia alone General Francisco Xavier Castaños (1756–1852) raised 30,000 men.

That the French should employ a heavy-handed policy in sacking several major towns only increased the numbers of volunteers flocking to join the new armies. The war took on an altogether wider scope when the insurgent juntas appealed to Britain for help through a delegation led by the Count de Toreño, who arrived in London on 8 June and was enthusiastically received. George Canning (1770–1827), the Foreign Secretary, promised weapons, ammunition and funds. Other regional emissaries followed and the time had now come to intervene. On 14 June Sir Arthur Wellesley was appointed to command an expeditionary force of 9,500 men. Ironically, these were originally intended for operations against Spain's colonies in South America, to reverse General Whitelocke's complete failure at Buenos Aires of the previous year.

As discussed earlier, since 1793 Britain had had mixed success in her amphibious operations on the Continent, with little impact on the overall course of the campaigns fought by her allies. The French invasion of Portugal and Spain at last provided an opening on the European mainland into which British military resources could be channeled, and in many ways this opening was ideal. First, Britain could exploit to the full her complete mastery of the seas by safely transporting troops and all the requisites of war; second, the Peninsula was accessible from three directions by sea, whereas practically everything the French army required – men and matériel – had by necessity to cross the Pyrenees. Finally, a British expeditionary force could operate in friendly country, a particularly important factor in a land inhospitable to large-scale military operations. Campaigning on friendly soil would also facilitate supply, communication and intelligence gathering.

Notwithstanding these considerable advantages for Britain, in military terms Spain herself was in a wretched state. Her best troops – 15,000 men under La Romana – remained in Denmark, while, as noted earlier, the remainder of the army consisted of underfed, ill-clothed and poorly paid men led by idle and incompetent officers and corrupt generals. Moreover, many of those who might have provided some element of cohesion and leadership backed Joseph's liberal policies and wished to discourage popular resistance, whatever its cause.

But if the French had little to fear from the regular Spanish forces, there were still considerable natural obstacles to overcome. Indeed, geography and climate could hardly have been more forbidding to an invader than in the Peninsula. High mountains with narrow defiles served as ideal places of ambush; primitive unpaved roads produced clouds of dust in the summer and became churned into mud in the winter; bitterly cold nights and blisteringly hot days tormented troops exposed both on the march and in camp; and passes choked with snow seriously impeded the progress of both man and horse. In vast stretches of the country the soil was so deficient in moisture and nutrient that it barely kept the inhabitants alive much less provided forage for hundreds of thousands of foreign troops. The French had no choice but to detach thousands of troops to protect their vital lines of communications back over the Pyrenees. These, in turn, were vulnerable, in Portugal and, especially, in Spain, to irregulars of various descriptions. Some were patriot guerrillas and others just plain bandits, who began to operate first as individuals, rising to small groups and finally to larger *partidas*, or bands, murdering stragglers, hounding foraging parties, and intercepting couriers.

Meanwhile, as the revolt spread and Spanish armies rose seemingly from nowhere, Napoleon took swift action against this wholly unexpected tide of resistance. From Bayonne he issued orders to destroy the juntas and their military forces. General Merle routed the Army of Estremadura under General Don Gregorio de la Cuesta (1740–1812) at Cabezon, but Marshal Bon Adrien de Moncey's (1754–1842) 9,000 men were ejected from Valencia, and when General Charles Lefebvre-Desnouëttes

(1773–1822) attempted to seize the key Aragonese city of Saragossa he encountered extraordinarily bitter resistance on the part of its brave inhabitants, led by the 28-year-old General José Palafox (1780–1847) and backed by a small contingent of regulars. When the French summoned him to surrender, Palafox, with great bravado, returned a curt 'War to the death!', and the bitter struggle went on with quarter neither asked nor given. Twice the garrison forced their assailants to abandon the siege, leaving 3,500 French dead. Also under siege was Gerona, in eastern Catalonia, where in July the inhabitants courageously held off 6,000 French troops, rising to 13,000 the following month.

Further reverses lay in store for the French. In July Cuesta assumed command of the Army of Galicia and, though the Spanish were utterly routed at Medina del Rio Seco

French capitulation at Bailen, 21 July 1808. While attempting to pacify Andalusia General Dupont, with 17,000 men, unexpectedly encountered overwhelming regular and irregular forces, which obliged him to surrender his entire force. Bailen held enormous political significance extending well beyond the Pyrenees, for in addition to lending heart to resistance in the Peninsula itself, it completely dispelled the myth prevalent throughout Europe that the French could not be beaten. (Roger-Viollet)

on the 14th, only nine days later General Pierre Dupont (1765–1840), finding his army of 17,500 men isolated at Bailen, deep in Andalusia, capitulated his entire force to Castaños on condition that they would be repatriated to France. The victors, however, treacherously murdered many of the prisoners and confined the remainder to almost inevitable death aboard the prison-hulks at Cadiz. Dupont's surrender had a dreadful effect on French morale and a correspondingly positive effect on that of his adversaries, for not since General Menou's surrender in Egypt in 1801 had a French army laid down its arms. French prestige, and above all the myth that the army was invincible, suffered a shattering blow. That these were, in the main, not the same men who had triumphed at Austerlitz, Jena, and Friedland mattered little. That they were Napoleonic soldiers was sufficient for contemporary observers to appreciate the significance of the French debacle.

Quite apart from attracting British attention, Bailen and the rapid creation of new Spanish armies seriously upset French plans, and without reinforcements readily available to protect Madrid, King Joseph withdrew northwards to the protection of the strategic line behind the River Ebro.

With remarkable rapidity, by the end of the summer of 1808, the Spanish had inflicted 40,000 casualties on the invaders and had driven them from most of the country. Joseph soon recognized that his task of ruling would be near impossible. Writing to the Emperor he declared despondently:

It would take 200,000 Frenchmen to conquer Spain and 10,000 scaffolds to maintain the prince who should be condemned to reign over them. No, sire, you do not know this people; each house will be a fortress, and every man of the same mind as the majority ... Not a Spaniard will be on my side if we are conquerors.

With cruel irony, Joseph evidently failed to realize that French troops in Spain already numbered 200,000, an impressive figure which, by October, would rise still further to 286,000 with the arrival of the reinforcements brought by Napoleon himself.

Arrival of the British

With the withdrawal of French troops behind the Ebro, Junot now lay isolated in distant Portugal where, though he faced insurrection rather than organized opposition as in Spain, his task was nonetheless an unenviable one. There were no Portuguese armies in the field, but holding down a seething population was not a task for which Napoleonic armies were trained. The situation worsened dramatically in August. Wellesley's expedition had left Cork on 13 July. His instructions from the Secretary of State for War told him to support the Portuguese and Spanish in 'throwing off the yoke of France, and [securing] the final and absolute evacuation of the Peninsula by the troops of France.'

Wellesley landed at Mondego Bay, 80 miles north of Lisbon, on 1 August and was joined four days later by 5,000 men conveyed from Cadiz by General Sir Brent Spencer (1760–1828). Wellesley began his march on the capital on the 10th, learning on the way that, though he was to be reinforced by another 15,000 men, he was to

be superceded in command by Lieutenant-General Sir Hew Dalrymple (1750–1830) and Lieutenant-General Sir Harry Burrard (1755–1813). Before this took effect, however, Wellesley achieved his first, though minor, victory at Roliça on 17 August, suffering 479 casualties to General Henri Delaborde's (1764–1833) 600 men and three guns. The army continued its march on Lisbon. Three days later Burrard arrived and, much to Wellesley's displeasure, ordered a halt. As Burrard was still aboard ship and therefore had not yet assumed command in the field, Wellesley was pleased to discover that Junot was in fact advancing against him from the south. He therefore took up defensive positions along a ridge and a hill at the village of Vimiero, near the mouth of the Maceira River.

At 9.00 am on the 21st Junot appeared and launched four attacks against Vimiero Hill, all of which Wellesley's infantry, deployed in line, repulsed with heavy loss. Two other attacks against the eastern ridge also failed, and when the battle ceased at midday the French had lost 1,000 men and 14 guns to Wellesley's 720. British morale soared and the route to Torres Vedras and the capital now lay unopposed. Nevertheless, Burrard, who now arrived on the scene, refused to permit Wellesley to follow up his victory, and the army halted to await the arrival of Lieutenant-General Sir John Moore. Junot therefore withdrew without interference, leaving Wellesley bitter at his superior's ineptitude. Still, the victory proved significant: Wellington had made excellent use of natural cover, temporarily deploying his infantry behind the crest of a hill to conceal its position and to protect it from artillery fire, before unleashing disciplined firepower at the head of advancing French columns. Properly handled, a two-rank British line could defeat the headlong French assaults which had hitherto proved so successful on battlefields across Europe. The superiority of French tactics had now been called into question.

Two days later Dalrymple and Junot opened negotiations for surrender. Failing to appreciate the full extent of Junot's predicament, Dalrymple concluded the

Battle of Vimiero, 21 August 1808: The first major action between British and French troops in the Peninsula, Vimiero demonstrated the superiority of the two-deep British line over the hitherto virtually invincible French column. By successfully opposing French skirmishers with his own screen of light infantry, which could protect his more vulnerable formed units, Wellington stripped the column of its main advantage: shock power against an enemy already demoralized by preparatory skirmish fire. Moreover, by deploying his men on the reverse side of the slope, Wellington effectively shielded his troops from artillery, while simultaneously concealing his dispositions and strength. (Madeley, Philip Haythornthwaite)

disgraceful Convention of Cintra on 31 August. This not only permitted Junot to evacuate his troops back to France, rather than confine them as prisoners of war, but also provided for their conveyance, together with all their weapons and booty, in British ships. Portugal would thus be freed of French troops, but such favorable terms granted to an army manifestly incapable of further resistance provoked a storm of public outcry in Britain which led the War Office to recall the three generals involved to face a court of inquiry. Only Wellesley survived the experience with his reputation intact, since he had shared no direct part in this lamentable arrangement. Nevertheless, on receiving no new command he returned, intensely disappointed, to his political duties in Dublin as Chief Secretary of Ireland.

In the meantime command of the 30,000 British troops in Portugal passed to Lieutenant-General Sir John Moore, an experienced commander who had established a solid reputation for efficiency, professionalism, and innovative reforms of

infantry tactics, above all, light infantry training, much of it carried out at Shornecliffe in the years immediately preceding the war. Moore was ordered to march into Spain to operate in conjunction with Spanish forces in driving the French out of the country. Accordingly, he began his advance in September, supported by another 15,000 under Major-General Sir David Baird (1757–1829), but his government's expectations were grossly unrealistic. The Spanish juntas had approximately 80,000 men in the field, but these were broken down into separate armies (of Galicia, Castile, Léon, Andalusia, Aragon, and Estremedura), each of which consisted of the poorly led, badly disciplined, ill-armed and ill-supplied rabble described earlier. To make matters worse, no coordinated plan existed between these armies, nor had the Spanish appointed a commander-in-chief with whom Moore could consult and cooperate. It soon became apparent that none of the various independent Spanish commanders was inclined to cooperate with, or properly supply, Moore.

Notwithstanding these serious disadvantages, on 18 October Moore began an advance on Burgos, where, in addition to joining Spanish forces watching the French across the Ebro, he planned to combine with the 10,000 men under Baird who had been transported to Corunna, on the northwest coast of Spain. Moore's army pushed on toward Salamanca over appalling roads, minus its complement of cavalry and artillery. Advised by the Spanish that the direct, northern route through Ciudad Rodrigo was impassable to artillery, Moore had sent them, under Sir John Hope (1765–1823), by an extremely circuitous southerly route via Badajoz and Madrid, to meet up with him in Salamanca. Worse still, Moore was as yet unaware that on 4 November Napoleon had arrived in Spain at the head of 125,000 men under his personal command, intent on expelling the British from the Peninsula and crushing the Spanish once and for all.

Incensed by Spanish resistance and the bunglings of his subordinates, the Emperor had shouted to Dumas: 'I can see very well that I must return and set the machine in motion again.' And from Erfurt on 13 October he wrote: 'The war must be terminated by a single *coup par manoeuvre* … My presence will be necessary.' Superior numbers led by the Emperor himself ought, Napoleon believed, to be more than sufficient to crush Spanish resistance decisively.

Accompanied by some of his greatest commanders, including Marshals Ney, Lannes, Jourdan, and Soult, and a host of other well-known generals, Napoleon and his *Grand Armée* opened an offensive on 6 November, sweeping aside all contenders, smashing the defenses at Burgos and arriving at Valladolid, midway to Madrid, on the 13th. At the same time Moore was reaching Salamanca, there to await Baird and Hope. From Valladolid Napoleon pushed on virtually unopposed toward the capital until, on the 30th he found the narrow defile at Somosierra blocked by 9,000 Spanish and a few pieces of artillery. Outflanking them was impossible without considerable delay. 'My Guard will not be stopped by peasants,' the Emperor declared, and, with scant regard for the lives of his men, ordered forward the 87 troopers of his Polish light cavalry escort in an attack that can only be described as suicidal. The horsemen, confined to a space only permitting four men to ride abreast, charged headlong into the guns, cut down the crews and galloped on to the crest, obliging the infantry to flee. The charge, followed up by further attacks by other units, succeeded, and passed into legend, but it cost the intrepid Poles half their number. The *Grande Armée* continued its inexorable advance, and entered Madrid on 4 December.

On 26 November, meanwhile, Moore learned that the bulk of Spanish forces had melted before the Emperor's advance. Thus abandoned by his inept allies to face the Napoleonic onslaught alone, Moore concluded that he must abandon attempts to advance on Burgos and order a withdrawal, a decision that met immediate and vociferous opposition not merely from the Spanish, but from his own subordinates and troops, who were itching to get to grips with the French.

Napoleon entering Spain, November 1808. Frustrated by the failure of his marshals to destroy the British Army, the Emperor determined to settle matters himself once and for all. 'The hideous leopard,' he announced to his soldiers in the flamboyant vocabulary reminiscent of his early campaigns in Italy and Egypt, 'contaminates by its presence the peninsula of Spain and Portugal. Let us carry our victorious Eagles to the Pillars of Hercules [Gibraltar].' (Roger-Viollet)

Moore found himself in a dreadful predicament: Hope arrived with the cavalry and artillery on 4 December, but Baird had reached no further than Astorga. Two days later, with enormous pressure building for him to continue the advance on Burgos and confront the French, Moore countermanded his orders for a withdrawal and again set the troops in motion. 'I was aware that I was risking infinitely too much,' he wrote, 'but something must be risked for the honour of the Service, and to make it apparent that we stuck to the Spaniards long after they had given up their cause for lost.'

A serious lack of intelligence left Moore unaware that Napoleon had entered Madrid on 4 December with an army of 80,000 men intent on destroying him. On the 11th Sir John therefore moved north with his meager 20,000 troops and finally linked up with Baird at Mayorga on the 20th, bringing his force up to 30,000. Two days later Napoleon, with the pick of his best troops, reached the snow-covered Guadarrama mountain range, whose high passes, though swept by a blizzard, he crossed with his army in pursuit of his still unsuspecting prey. All seemed well to Moore when, on Christmas Eve, with all his forces finally united, his army was *en route* for Carrion, where Marshal Nicolas Soult (1769–1851) lay temptingly vulnerable with a mere 16,000 men. Late that evening, however, Moore learned of Napoleon's advance from a captured dispatch. Now aware of the vastly superior forces threatening him, the British commander had no option but to order a general retreat.

The retreat to Corunna

Moore hoped to confront Soult's army before it combined forces with that under Junot, but when on 4 December he learned that Madrid had fallen, he concluded that the Spanish would never materialize to support him. With Napoleon in pursuit, Moore began a desperate winter retreat to Corunna on Christmas Day. Conducted over icy and snow-bound roads and abysmal mountain tracks, the march became a nightmare as discipline broke down and men collapsed from hunger, cold and exhaustion. The sick and wounded had to be left behind in the villages through which the army passed or sometimes literally abandoned on the roadside to face inevitable death from hunger or exposure, all for the lack of transport or strength to carry them. The rearguard, the elite Light Brigade, initially under Brigadier-General Robert 'Black Bob' Craufurd (1764–1812) and later Major-General Edward Paget (1775–1849), nonetheless offered a magnificent defense against the French van whenever it made contact, always managing to keep it at bay and allowing the main body to escape. The cavalry, under Lord Henry Paget (1768–1854) (Edward's brother), also played a vital role in holding back the pursuers. As the retreat progressed, much of Moore's formations disintegrated into a mere rabble which took to pillage and drink; in one instance, the column was obliged to abandon 1,000 drunken soldiers in the village of Bembibre, where most were massacred where they lay by French cavalry. One senior commissary officer observed that:

All orderly distribution was at an end. No officer or non-commissioned officer was respected … every soldier took what he liked, everything was plundered, carried away and trampled under foot … Although Villafranca is not small, every corner of it was soon full of men …Fresh troops were always streaming in, the stores of depots were also violently raided … In the end Villafranca was literally plundered, and the drunkenness that prevailed … led to the most shameful incidents.

Later during the retreat he added:

The road was strewn with dead horses, bloodstained snow, broken carts, scrapped ammunition boxes, cases, spiked guns, dead mules, donkeys and dogs, starved and frozen soldiers, women [soldiers' wives] and children … Discipline became ever more and more relaxed … Every hour the misery of the troops increased.

All along the route to Corunna the army trudged through knee-deep snow and mud with a line of frozen bodies marking the passage of the retreat.

On the 30th the army reached Astorga, 200 miles (322 km) from Corunna, where it was possible to stand and fight. Moore concluded, nevertheless, that a victory would achieve nothing, while a defeat would certainly destroy his demoralized army. Against bitter opposition from his generals, who advocated a stand, he therefore decided to press on, first dividing his force and sending south to Vigo the 3,500 men of the Light Brigade and the King's German Legion. Napoleon had meanwhile passed command of the army on to Soult, while he himself returned to quash political intrigue brewing in Paris. Though the Emperor promised to return to Spain he never did, and the conquest of the country was left in the hands of men who would never, for reasons which will become clear later, complete this formidable task.

At last, on 11 January 1809, Moore's ragged but unbroken army – they had not lost a single gun or color – reached Corunna, where Shaumann saw the shattered remnant

of men '… all in tatters, hollow eyed, and covered with blood and filth. They looked so terrible that the people made the sign of the cross as they passed …' The promised transports were not yet in the harbor, but, fortunately for Moore, by the time Soult's main body of 20,000 (with the same number *en route*) appeared, the ships had arrived and an orderly disembarkation was already under way, covered by a force of 15,000 men and 12 guns. Soult attacked on 16 January in a pitched battle outside the town, in the course of which Moore, at the cost of his own life, first repulsed and then drove back his assailants several miles. By dusk the fighting was over, with 800 British casualties, including the much-loved Sir John, whom his men interred in the ramparts of the city. The embarkation duly continued and was completed on the 19th, when the remnants of the army sailed for England.

On its surface the campaign appeared to have ended in unmitigated disaster for the British, having cost them 6,000 men and a large quantity of weapons and equipment. The French remained in possession of most of Spain and Portugal and the British government, under the Duke of Portland, was justifiably reluctant to undertake any future offensive operations. On the other hand, notwithstanding their relentless

Battle of Corunna, 16 January 1809. Following its horrific retreat from Sahagun, Sir John Moore's army reached the northwest coast of Spain with the French close in pursuit. Soult nevertheless unwisely chose to concentrate his forces before launching an attack, thus providing Moore with a two-day respite in which to rest, re-supply and evacuate much of his army by sea. Sir John's superb defense, which cost him his own life, obliged the French to retire and enabled the remaining British troops to embark without further harassment. (Ann Ronan Picture Library)

pursuit, the French had failed to destroy Moore's army, and though it had endured a terrible campaign, its march and subsequent retreat was to shape the future course of the war decisively. In short, by continuing his advance on Burgos, Moore had obliged Napoleon to focus his attention on the British rather than the Spanish forces. This provided the British vital time with which to consolidate their defenses in Portugal and their Spanish allies with an opportunity to recuperate and prepare for the next campaign season. The vital British base at Lisbon was therefore preserved and the French had yet to conquer southern Spain. Moore's actions, therefore, may well have prevented a complete French victory by the end of 1808.

But if the French had found themselves unable to destroy Moore's army, they were nevertheless successful elsewhere, utterly

Retreat to Corunna

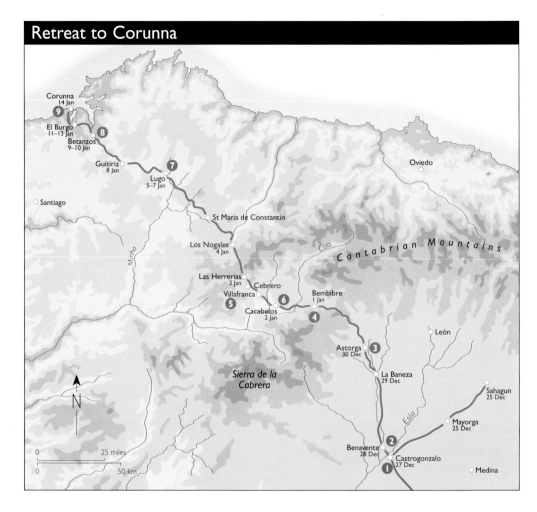

1. Castrogonzalo. Moore crosses River Esla, blowing the bridge behind him. Enters Galician mountains.
2. Benavente. Demoralized by retreating rather than facing the French in battle, troops loot and pillage the town. On 29 December 600 Imperial Guard cavalry are defeated by British cavalry, losing almost 200.
3. Astorga. Moore chooses not to stand; detaches two brigades by different routes to Vigo.
4. Bembibre. Troops raid wine cellars and get exceedingly drunk. 1,000 left behind are mostly massacred by French cavalry.
5. Villafranca. Starving vanguard raids depot containing fortnight's supply of food.
6. Cacebelos. Moore's rearguard puts up stiff resistance against Soult's pursuing vanguard.
7. Lugo. Moore halts and prepares to fight, but Soult refuses to oblige him.
8. Betanzos. Troops emerge from the mountains.
9. Corunna. Survivors reach their destination after a 312 mile (499km) march. Royal Navy transports arrive 14 January. Embarkation begins immediately. Soult defeated outside town on 16th, but Moore killed.

crushing the Spanish at Ucles in January and at Medellin in March. Defeating in open battle the sometimes sizable though nevertheless feeble regular armies of the juntas was no great challenge for veteran French forces, but siege operations proved altogether more vicious and bloody undertakings. Nowhere was this more true than in the capital city of Aragon, Saragossa, whose people, supported by a contingent of regular troops and large numbers of the local peasantry, grimly resisted the siege laid against them in December. As Marbot recalled:

The town was surrounded by immense and solidly built convents; these were fortified and guns placed in them. All the houses were loopholed [the walls being perforated to facilitate small arms fire] and the streets barricaded;

powder, cannon-balls, and bullets were manufactured, and great stores of food collected. All the inhabitants enrolled themselves ... The besieged only agreed on one point: to defend themselves to the death ... Religious fanaticism and the sacred love of country exalted their courage, and they blindly resigned themselves to the will of God.

In the course of two months the city was reduced by sappers employing a systematic combination of mining and desperate assaults. 'Never have I seen such keen determination,' Marshal Lannes informed the Emperor by dispatch. 'I have seen women come to be killed in the breach. Every house has to be taken by storm ...' At last, on 20 February, after a horrendous trial in which the citizens, even in the midst of starvation and disease, had engaged in savage house-to-house fighting at a total cost exceeding 50,000 lives, fewer than half of whom were soldiers, the city capitulated. Such instances of unmatched civilian resistance highlighted the incompetence of the regular Spanish armies and marked a new and dreadful chapter in

Manuela Sanchez, the 'Maid of Saragossa'. After the crew of a cannon, including her fiancé, was wiped out by French fire, she boldly lit the fuse with a party of advancing infantry only yards away. Thousands of Spanish women took an active part in civilian resistance, particularly in the defense of cities like Saragossa and Gerona. Most tended the wounded, cooked, and brought forward ammunition and water, but others took up arms beside the men. (Ann Ronan Picture Library)

warfare. If any single episode in the Peninsular War symbolized Spanish defiance, it was the siege of Saragossa.

Operations in 1809

Despite the evacuation of Moore's army the British government decided to continue the war in support of Portugal, where 16,000 British troops still remained defending Lisbon. Renewed effort came in the form of a second expeditionary force, dispatched in April under Wellesley, who, delighted by his return, had prepared an 'Appreciation of the Situation' for his superiors in which he had laid out the clear strategy that was to guide him for the remainder of the war. Since the government was only prepared to commit a small force, Wellesley had to assure ministers that he could defend Portugal with 20,000 British troops in conjunction with a reorganized Portuguese army. Protecting Portugal, he argued, could be achieved provided that Spain continued to resist occupation and supported Britain's efforts. He further maintained that Spain's sheer size and the ferocity of her population to foreign occupation would make it impossible for the French to subdue the country entirely.

Wellesley's strategy also depended on continued British control of the sea and, critically – and this could not be guaranteed – he had at all costs to preserve his small force from defeat or severe loss, whether in action or from disease. This highly uncertain condition, Sir Arthur argued, partly depended on his being able to prevent the French from concentrating overwhelming strength against him. Finally, he concluded, severe supply difficulties, exacerbated by overextended lines of communication, and coupled with continuous attacks by partisans, would all hamper the French and favor his own prospects for defending Portugal and eventually carrying the campaign into the heart of Spain.

Wellesley landed at Lisbon on 22 April, a mere three months after Moore's army had embarked at Corunna. The British controlled southern Portugal, but to the north Marshal Soult, with 20,000 men, controlled the area from Coimbra stretching north, including the important coastal town of Oporto. With exceptional speed Wellesley reorganized his army in an effort to improve its mobility and fighting capability. Chief amongst the changes he introduced was the amalgamation of his various brigades into divisions which, with their own commanders and staff, could operate with considerably more independence than hitherto. He also began to rebuild the Portuguese army, placing British officers at all levels of command and assigning a Portuguese battalion to each of his exclusively British brigades. Thus began a

process which, over the course of the next several years, would witness the rapid growth of competently trained and led Portuguese forces as an integral part of the allied effort.

Within a fortnight of his arrival Wellesley's preparations were complete. He was ready to march against one of the three armies opposing him: Marshal Soult in the north, General Pierre Lapisse (1762–1809) near Ciudad Rodrigo, and Marshal Claude Victor (1764–1841) to the south at Talavera. Both Lapisse and Victor could cross into Portugal, and were the three forces to combine, Wellesley would face double his own numbers. On the other hand, the French armies were separated by considerable distances and rough terrain, and Wellesley confidently believed he could defeat each in turn before they could oppose him as a combined force. He intended to confront Soult first, ejecting him from Portugal before confronting Victor in the south. Thus, leaving 12,000 troops under General Mackenzie to defend Lisbon, and sending 6,000 men under General William Beresford (1764–1854) to march east to block Soult's line of retreat, he set out on 8 May with 16,000 British, 2,400 Portuguese and 24 guns. His object was to cross the River Douro at Oporto, which Soult had occupied on 29 March.

Reaching the Douro early on 12 May, Wellesley discovered Soult ensconced on the opposite side, having destroyed the only bridge across the river and moved every boat to the north bank. Confident that he was protected from an attack across the river, the French commander was therefore caught completely unprepared when Wellesley boldly ferried several hundred men across in barges – wine-barges, appropriately enough in this city – provided by the populace. By the time the French discovered the presence of the British, their chance of driving them into the water was lost, and every counterattack was repulsed. Further upstream meanwhile, at Avintas, more British troops effected a crossing, preventing Soult and his 11,000 men from withdrawing in that direction. The best route of escape lay to the east, blocked by Beresford; Soult therefore had no option but to leave behind most of his transport and retreat into the mountains to the north.

The crossing of the Douro and the victory at Oporto demonstrated Wellesley's ability to act boldly and decisively, and to conceive and execute plans with little preparation time. As a result, the French were forced to abandon Portugal for a second time, having sustained heavy losses in men and equipment. The resulting blow to French morale gave a boost to the Allies, and with Soult out of the way Wellesley was free to proceed south against Victor. Elsewhere, the French, finding themselves constantly under guerrilla attack, as well as by La Romana's regulars, withdrew from Galicia.

Wellesley's operations in Spain were now to involve him in collaboration with the military forces of that country. This posed a number of problems, for without any unified command the Spanish armies had no coherent strategy, leaving Wellesley unable to coordinate his efforts with the various Spanish generals in the field, each of whom jealously operated on his own terms with little inclination to support his own colleagues, much less Wellesley. Yet operating on Spanish soil obliged the British commander-in-chief to cooperate with the Spanish generals, insofar as they permitted it, in particular with Cuesta. Thirty years Wellesley's senior, ill-tempered, stubborn, and utterly unfit to command, Cuesta neither trusted Wellesley nor wished to accept his advice, and only communicated through his own chief of staff. Rifleman Harris described him as 'that deformed-looking lump of pride, ignorance and treachery … He was the most murderous-looking old man I ever saw.' If Cuesta were not bad enough, the junta was worse, having promised Wellesley food and transport which in the end never materialized.

On 10 July, with his army of 20,000 at Plasencia, Wellesley met with Cuesta, who was in command of 35,000 men, to negotiate a joint strategy. Relations between the two were prickly, but they nonetheless agreed to join forces at Oropesa and to move their combined 55,000 troops against Victor's much smaller force of 22,000 at Talavera. The French had other forces, in Madrid and just south of the capital, but measures were taken to try to prevent them from uniting with Victor. Thus, on 21 July, British and Spanish forces united as agreed and Cuesta, as planned, proceeded towards Victor's position at the River Alberche, while Wellesley stood in reserve. The two allied generals agreed to attack together on the 23rd, but when at sunrise Wellesley's forces were ready to open the engagement, the Spanish were nowhere to be seen. Wellesley found their commander three hours later, sleeping soundly. When awakened Cuesta announced that his troops were too tired to attack, and by this off-hand and unaccountable manner a splendid opportunity was thus lost to the allied cause. Wellesley, livid, not least because lack of the promised Spanish supplies had left his troops without adequate food for two days, was powerless to stop Victor from withdrawing, which that marshal did that evening entirely unopposed.

In a bizarre move Cuesta then decided to follow the French on his own, and on the 24th he proceeded towards the capital, only to be confronted and routed on the following day at Alcabon by 46,000 French, who then pursued him to the Alberche. Local circumstances had suddenly shifted in favor of the French, who now possessed a united force comprising both King Joseph's forces and those of Marshal Victor, which had been brought together in order to defeat Cuesta. Together these well outnumbered Wellesley, who was obliged quickly to take up a defensive position. At this Wellesley was clearly adept, and he accordingly chose a strong post north of the town of Talavera. Firmly fixed, he awaited the inevitable attack.

Wellesley had a theoretical strength of 55,000, but only 20,000 of these, plus 36 guns, were his own troops, the remaining being Cuesta's unreliable Spanish. The army under King Joseph was composed of 46,000 troops and 86 guns – twice the size of the British and King's German Legion (KGL) force. The French attacked the allied left on the night of the 27th, but were repulsed. They resumed the offensive on the following day, when several thousand Spanish ran off at the outset of the fighting. The French

Charge of the 48th Foot at Talavera. The collapse of
Sherbrooke's division in the course of the fighting left an
enormous gap in the British line that threatened the
whole army with imminent defeat. Unable to spare an
entire brigade from the Cerro de Medellin, Wellesley
deployed only the 800-strong 48th Foot and two
regiments of Light Dragoons as a temporary plug. The
48th lost nearly a quarter of its strength in killed and
wounded – not untypical of Napoleonic battles.
(Ann Ronan Picture Library)

assaulted several points along Wellesley's
line, but successive attacking columns were
driven off by British volleys, and at last the
French withdrew.

Lieutenant Simmons recorded the
appalling sight of the field of Talavera in the
aftermath of the carnage:

Thousands dead and dying in every direction,
horses, men, French and English, in whole lines
who had cut each other down and I am sorry to say
the Spaniards butchering the wounded French-men
at every opportunity and stripping them naked.

The following day his brigade was assigned
the unenviable job of 'collecting the dead
bodies and putting them into large heaps
mixed with faggots and burning them. The

stench from so many dead bodies was volatile
and offensive beyond conception as the heat
of the weather was very great.' The sound of
the wounded was dreadful, as well. August
Schaumann, a British commissary officer,
encountered a convent in the town
requisitioned as a hospital:

Never shall I forget the heart-rending cries which
could be heard coming from the windows … [from
one of which] … the amputated arms and legs were
being flung out upon a small square below. In front
of the door lay the wounded, who had been
deposited there as fast as they arrived, awaiting
their turn. Many of them were already dead.

The defensive tactics employed by Wellesley
at Talavera proved, like those used at Roliça and
Vimiero, to be highly effective against massed
French columns of attack. British skirmishers
had shown themselves to be the match of their
French counterparts: Wellesley had once again
positioned his men behind the crest of a hill to
shield them from the more numerous French
artillery, and, most significantly, once again a
pitched battle revealed the superiority of the
British line against the French column. Infantry
firepower, when withheld until the attacker was

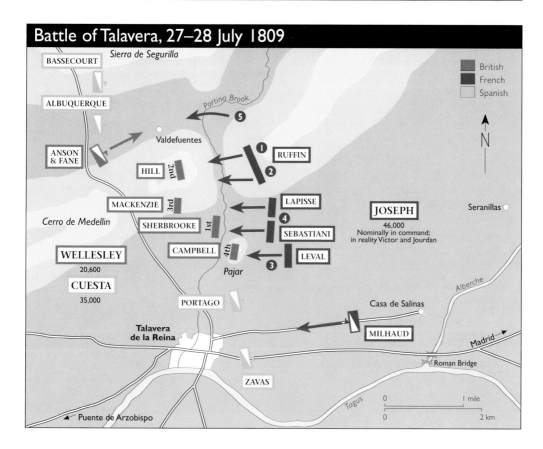

Battle of Talavera, 27–28 July 1809

1. 27 July 9.00 pm. As a prelude to the main action to open on the 28th, Ruffin launches a surprise night attack against a ridge called the Cerro de Medellin and narrowly fails to take it.
2. 5.00 am 28 July. After an intense bombardment by 53 guns, Ruffin's division of 4,300 again attacks Hill's position on the Medellin; repulsed with heavy losses from musketry by infantry deployed in line. Informal truce of several hours follows.
3. 1.15 pm. As a diversion for the main attack to be made against the Medellin, Leval assaults Campbell's 4th Division on the Pajar, but is repulsed.
4. 1.30 pm. After a bombardment by 80 guns, Sebastiani and Lapisse launch main thrust, but are repulsed.
5. 2.40 pm. Ruffin attacks again. British cavalry charge.

close at hand and immediately followed by a spirited bayonet charge, had proved devastatingly effective. Lastly, Wellesley had made himself conspicuous to his troops under fire, constantly moving from one section to another, encouraging the men, issuing orders directly and observing the progress of the fighting.

Having said this, Wellesley's achievement, though a victory, was dearly bought,

costing a quarter of his effective strength (5,300 casualties) compared to the French, who lost less than a fifth of theirs, or 7,200. Though French losses were higher in absolute terms, they could afford these much more than could Wellesley, who also suffered a particular shortage of cavalry at this time. Indeed, numerical inferiority, especially in terms of cavalry and artillery, would constantly plague the Allied war effort in the Peninsula, and it would become a testament to Wellesley's eventual greatness that he consistently devised successful methods and strategies to compensate for these deficiencies. News of the victory created a sensation back in Britain, whose hero was raised to the peerage as Viscount Wellington.

Despite his victory at Talavera, Wellington could not afford to be complacent. He withdrew across the Tagus when, on 3 August, he was informed that an army of 50,000 under Soult was marching south from Salamanca in a bid to block his communications with

Portugal. On the 20th he retreated still further, to Badajoz, on the Spanish-Portuguese border, from which he could defend the southern route to Lisbon. The retreat was a dreadful affair; not, perhaps, comparable to Corunna, but Wellington's troops suffered badly from shortages of food. Refuge just over the border in Portugal would have suited Wellington better, but, recognizing the importance of preserving the delicate Anglo-Spanish relationship, he remained on Spanish territory.

Wellington well appreciated that the war would not be won overnight and that he must take a long-term view of the situation. The French might yet invade Portugal a third time, and if they did so with sufficient strength the Allied armies could not, unaided, hold back the tide. Therefore, in October, to compensate for his numerical inferiority he devised what in time would prove a brilliant plan of defense. In that month he left the army cantonment in Spain and, in the company of his engineers, surveyed the area around Lisbon. After extensive planning they devised a scheme for a series of fortifications which, in three lines, were to run north and west of Lisbon and to be manned by a small contingent of British troops and tens of thousands of Portuguese militia, known as the *Ordenenza*. These defensive works were to become the famous Lines of Torres Vedras. Work began immediately, and tens of thousands of Portuguese laborers toiled to construct the Lines, a task which occupied them for the next 12 months. So effective was the veil of secrecy surrounding the project that the French would have no inkling of its existence until they actually arrived before the Lines towards the end of the following year.

Having safely ensconced himself in and around Badajoz, Wellington did not undertake any major operations for the remainder of the year, and so incensed was he with the antics of his Spanish allies that he adamantly declined to operate jointly with them. They had failed to seize the opportunity to defeat the French in July and when, a few days later, Wellington was confronted alone at Talavera, he had been lucky to withstand the assault. Worse still, even while the British were in the midst of the

battle, fleeing Spanish soldiers had looted British baggage wagons in the rear. Nor had Wellington received the promised supplies and food. In short, he was unwilling to jeopardize his army when the Spanish had repeatedly proven themselves both incompetent and unreliable. 'Till the evils of which I think I have reason to complain are remedied ...,' he wrote in agitation, 'I cannot enter into any system of co-operation with the Spanish Army.'

Still, to their considerable credit, the Spanish continued to fight on, albeit independently, and defeated the French at Alcaniz on 23 May and again on 18 October at Tamames. But these successes, like those few before them, were short-lived. They were defeated at Almonacid on 10 August and, on 19 November, 52,000 Spanish commanded by General Areizago were routed at Ocaña, losing 18,000 men, 50 guns and 30 colors. Only 10 days later, at Alba de Tormes, they were trounced again, with 3,000 casualties to the tiny loss to the French of just 300. Moreover, on 11 December Gerona finally surrendered after an eight-month siege – another epic defense, albeit on a somewhat smaller scale than Saragossa. Such consistent Spanish reverses put the French in a better position to threaten Portugal, leaving Wellington little option but to re-cross the border on 9 December and await the new season for campaigning in the spring.

If Spain's fortunes appeared to be on the wane, for Wellington the campaign of 1809 ended on a fairly satisfactory note. With a small army he had, in consequence of Oporto, evicted the French from Portugal for the second time, and though his campaign in Spain had miscarried, he had managed to defeat his opponent's counteroffensive at Talavera. His army remained intact, its morale, training, and efficiency were constantly rising, and Beresford's reforms were gradually taking effect in the Portuguese ranks, though they had not yet been tested in action. As for the Spanish, though their armies continued to suffer successive defeats, they always returned to the contest, diverting sizable French forces from operating against Wellington or subduing the guerrillas, and inflicting casualties in battle.

Operations in 1810

With the end of Napoleon's campaign against Austria, culminating in the Battle of Wagram on 5–6 July 1809, substantial numbers of French troops could be shifted for service in the Peninsula. By early 1810 there were 325,000 men in Spain – far more than the Allies. With peace reigning throughout the Napoleonic Empire except in Spain, Joseph ought to have had greater success; but holding down an entire hostile population was proving impossible. 'My power does not extend beyond Madrid,' he complained to the Emperor, 'and at Madrid itself I am daily thwarted … I am only King of Spain by the force of your arms.' To Napoleon winning the hearts and minds of the Spanish by the introduction of liberal political and social reforms was not the answer. Only a military solution would suffice: 'You will not succeed in Spain except by vigour and energy. This parade of goodness and clemency ends in nothing.'

Wellington, of course, faced his own problems. French forces outnumbered him by many times and against such odds he had to remain on the defensive. His policy was severely criticized by both the British and Spanish governments for his apparent inactivity, yet he wisely spent the first nine months of the year preparing his army and the country for an anticipated third invasion of Portugal. A French advance could come from three possible directions: from the center down the River Tagus, where Wellington placed Beresford's Portuguese troops; from the south via Badajoz, where he put Sir Rowland Hill with 7,000 British and 13,000 Portuguese; or from the north, through Ciudad Rodrigo and Almeida, which Wellington thought was the most likely direction of attack. Therefore, he marched his remaining troops to protect this route. In front of this position the Light Division provided both a screen for the army and intelligence on French movements. These tasks they performed extremely well, and the French were unable to probe Wellington's position to assess his strength or dispositions.

Wellington spent much of his time improving his defense, his intelligence network and in reorganization and training. At the same time Beresford continued to improve and expand the Portuguese forces under his command, and in the course of the year he integrated whole Portuguese brigades into most of the all-British/KGL divisions. He also improved and expanded the Portuguese militia, thus freeing up regular troops for service in the line. In addition to relying on Portuguese and Spanish guerrillas and other civilians for intelligence, Wellington also acquired information from his own intelligence officers, sent deep behind hostile lines to gather information on French strength and dispositions. And, as part of his general defensive measures in Portugal, he received permission from Portuguese officials to implement a policy of what would now be known as 'scorched earth'; in short, should the French actually invade as expected, they would find themselves deprived of crops, equipment and transport. Throughout this period the construction of the Lines of Torres Vedras continued steadily, supervised by the Chief Engineer, Lieutenant Colonel Sir Richard Fletcher (1768–1813), all unbeknown to the French.

It was now only a matter of time before he would confront the French in battle, and as he was to do many years later at Waterloo, Wellington set out to select a particularly strong defensive position for just such a purpose. The direction of his adversary's approach was, of course, unknown, but it became immediately obvious to the British C-in-C that if the French obliged him, the 11 mile (18 km) long, 1,000 ft (315 m) ridge at Busaco would be an ideal position to defend, rising as it did extremely sharply from its base. On the reverse side of the summit he therefore constructed a road running the length of the ridge, thus facilitating the movement of troops from one sector of the battlefield to another – completely out of sight of the attacker.

The French were not idle during this period. In April 1810 Napoleon sent Marshal

Masséna to the Peninsula with orders to reconquer Portugal. This clear objective notwithstanding, the French system of command would nevertheless continue to be hampered by the absence of an overall commander in Spain and the consequent necessity of communicating with Paris. This was a time-consuming and expensive practice which often meant that changing circumstances rendered reports and orders completely obsolete by the time they were issued or received.

The campaign opened in May when Masséna proceeded to besiege the vital border fortress of Ciudad Rodrigo, which controlled the northern corridor between Spain and Portugal. The fortress, held by 5,500 Spanish troops under Herrasti, surrendered on 10 July. Against the wishes of the Spanish government as well as his own troops, Wellington had refused to come to the city's relief, as the risks seemed clearly to outweigh the benefits. But British forces were not wholly inactive, for a fortnight later Marshal Michel Ney (1769–1815), with 24,000 troops, advanced and fought the Light Division, which narrowly escaped disaster along the rocky banks of the River Coa. The Portuguese counterpart to Ciudad Rodrigo was Almeida, another strong fortress, but it fell prematurely when on 26 August French artillery fire ignited loose powder, causing a catastrophic explosion in the magazine that left 500 dead and obliged the garrison commander to capitulate on the 28th. With the fall of Ciudad Rodrigo and Almeida the French had succeeded in opening the northern invasion route between the two countries. Nonetheless, Wellington had reason for some hope, for when Masséna finally continued his march west on 15 September, he chose precisely the route that Wellington had hoped and marched straight toward the ridge at Busaco.

Wellington duly positioned his troops according to the plans he had devised months before and summoned the 20,000 men under Hill to reinforce him. That completed, Wellington had a formidable 52,000 men, half of whom were

RIGHT Busaco demonstrated not only the superiority of the British line versus the French column but the benefits of a strong defensive position, even without earthworks.
1. 5.45 am Merle's division (11 btns) attacks in column; repulsed.
2. 6.00 am Heudelet attacks with four battalions; also repulsed, in part by spirited charge of the 88th Foot (Connaught Rangers).
3. 6.00 am Foy attacks Picton's 3rd Division with seven battalions north of San Antonio; repulsed.
4. 8.15 am Loison attacks with 12 battalions (6,000), unaware that the Lt Div. (1,800) lay behind the crest; also repulsed with a loss of 1,200.
5. 9.00 am Marchand attacks with 11 battalions versus Packs' Portuguese Brigade; repulsed.

now Portuguese, as against 65,000 French. Though outnumbered, Wellington had had more than a year to train his troops, and though the Portuguese were as yet untried, they too had undergone extensive training. On 27 September Masséna flung his columns against the ridge in wave after wave, all to no avail. Every assault was repulsed and the Portuguese, for their part, fought creditably. Rather than pursue his beaten foe, Wellington implemented the strategy he had planned for just such a situation: withdrawal to the protection of the Lines of Torres Vedras, destroying everything in his path that could be of use to the French. The army suffered less during this withdrawal than during the retreats of 1809, but the civilians who accompanied it underwent terrible hardships: Schaumann noted in his diary that

The retreat … from Coimbra to the fortified lines presented a sad spectacle. The roads were littered with smashed cases and boxes, broken wagons and carts, dead horses and exhausted men. Every division was accompanied by a body of refugees as great as itself and rich and poor alike, either walking, or mounted on horses or donkeys, were to be seen all higgledy-piggledy – men and women, young and old, mothers leading children, or carrying them on their backs, nuns who had left their convents, and, quite strange to the world, either wandered about helplessly, beside themselves with fear, looking timidly for their relations, or else, grown bold, linked arms with the soldiers and carried the

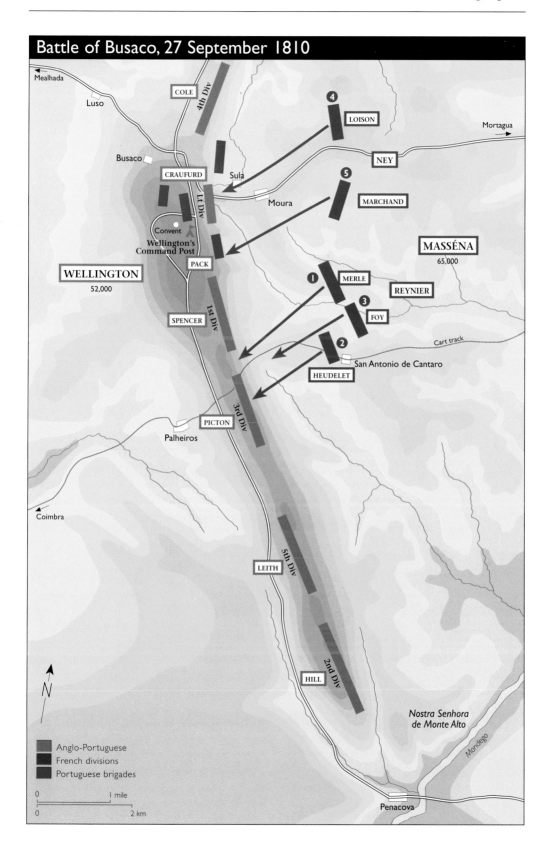

Battle of Busaco, 27 September 1810

Mealhada
Luso
Busaco
COLE
4th Div
LOISON
④
Mortagua
NEY
Sula
CRAUFURD
Moura
MARCHAND
⑤
Lt Div
Convent
Wellington's
Command Post
PACK
MASSÉNA
65,000
WELLINGTON
52,000
MERLE
①
REYNIER
③
FOY
SPENCER
1st Div
②
San Antonio de Cantaro
Cart track
HEUDELET
PICTON
Palheiros
3rd Div
Coimbra
LEITH
5th Div
HILL
2nd Div
Nostra Senhora
de Monte Alto
Mondego

Anglo-Portuguese
French divisions
Portuguese brigades

0   1 mile
0   2 km

Penacova

Battle of Busaco, 27 September 1810. French infantry struggling uphill against severe artillery and small arms fire. At one point they could see nothing but the lone figure of Major-General Robert 'Black Bob' Craufurd, commander of the Light Division, unaware that concealed in a sunken road behind him lay the 43rd and 52nd Foot. As the attackers approached the summit Craufurd turned round and cried, 'Now Fifty Second! Avenge Moore!' With a mighty 'Huzza!' the 52nd bounded forward with the bayonet, forcing the French to flee in disorder. (Roger-Viollet)

latter's knapsacks. Monks, priests and invalids – everybody was taking flight. The nearer the procession came to Lisbon, the greater the number of animals belonging to the refugees that fell dead either from fatigue or hunger; and very soon the ladies were to be seen wading in torn silk shoes, or barefoot through the mud. Despair was written on all faces.

Masséna accepted the bait and followed closely on Allied heels, still unaware of the existence of the Lines until they hove into view on 10 October. These fortifications had been constructed with such skill that they required only 2,500 British troops,

25,000 Portuguese militia and 8,000 Spanish regulars to defend them. The French marshal recognized their strength immediately, but sought confirmation by probing them on the 14th. This proved a costly failure, and with no prospect of penetrating the defenses Masséna declined to try again. Instead he established his camp to their front, hoping to coax Wellington out. But he prudently remained in place, well fed and supplied by the Royal Navy. Masséna, by contrast, with his supplies exhausted and facing the devastation deliberately wrought on the countryside by Wellington's retreating troops, was forced to withdraw to Santarem on 15 November. Wellington emerged from the Lines and advanced by degrees, but chose not to attack, for he dared not risk his army until the opportunity was right. His strategy proved successful, for starvation and disease that winter cost the French 25,000 men – all without a fight. Thus, the Lines of Torres Vedras had served their purpose brilliantly, completely frustrating French hopes of taking Lisbon, and rendering northern Portugal effectively untenable.

Operations in 1811

While Masséna's men languished on meager rations at Santarem, Wellington's army remained in complete safety and well supplied in its camps behind the Lines of Torres Vedras. Soult continued his siege of Badajoz, while other forces captured Olivenza on 22 January and defeated the Spanish at the Gebora River on 19 February. As for the Anglo-Portuguese, the year 1811 was to be a more active one for these forces than the previous year, with three pitched battles: Barrosa (5 March), Fuentes de Oñoro (3–5 May), and Albuera (16 May), two of which would be fought by Wellington's subordinates.

Since January 1810 an Anglo-Spanish force of 26,000 had been besieged in Cadiz, in the extreme south of the country and the seat of the Supreme Junta. In February 1811 the commander decided to use 13,000 of these in an attack by land and sea against the investing army. But General La Peña, leading the Spanish contingent, bungled the operation, leaving Sir Thomas Graham's 5,000 British troops unsupported at Barrosa, where on 5 March Marshal Victor struck

with 9,000 troops. Despite numerical inferiority Graham risked everything in a daring counterattack and succeeded.

That same day Masséna, unable to confront Wellington while he remained behind the Lines, incapable of feeding his starving and disease-ridden army around Santarem in a region devastated by the Allied policy of 'scorched earth', and continually dogged by guerrilla activity, began withdrawing his dejected men into Spain, reaching Salamanca on 11 April. In the process he had had to leave behind most of his transport and had lost 25,000 out of the 65,000 men with which he had started the campaign, fewer than half of whose losses were accounted for by battle losses and prisoners. Thus the Lines of Torres Vedras

Torres Vedras, the main area around which Wellington ordered construction of what proved to be impregnable 'Lines' extending across Portugal from the River Tagus to the Atlantic. The Lines served two purposes: to prevent the French from taking the vital supply base at Lisbon, and to enable Wellington time in which to evacuate the country in the event of unforeseen disaster. They proved brilliantly successful in 1810–1811. Here French troops are shown engaged in an unsuccessful probe near Agraco on 14 October 1810. (Ann Ronan Picture Library)

proved exceptionally cost effective to the
Allies. As soon as Masséna had begun his
retreat from Santarem the Allies followed,
amused by the straw dummy sentries which
the French had left behind to try to trick
them. Except for the garrison at Almeida, the
French had now been forced out of Portugal
for the third time.

Nonetheless, Soult had managed to effect
the surrender of the key frontier city of
Badajoz on 10 March, and with its possession
and that of Ciudad Rodrigo, the French held
both routes connecting Spain and Portugal.
In order to defend the latter, Wellington had
therefore to observe both cities, thus dividing
his small army of 58,000 by 120 miles
(193 km). Masséna and Soult, were they able
to join their respective forces, could mass a
minimum of 70,000 men. With his forces
divided and his lines of communications
dangerously long, Wellington established
38,000 men under himself at Frenada in the
north, while General Beresford, with 20,000,
marched south. On 25 March Beresford
defeated the French in a minor action at
Campo Mayor and the following month he
besieged Badajoz, though without a siege
train the prospects of success were very slim
indeed. Wellington advised Beresford, should
Soult attack him, to consider establishing his
defense at Albuera, a village 14 miles
southeast of Badajoz.

At the beginning of May Masséna led his
48,000 troops west, with the intention of
relieving the garrison at Almeida, the only
French troops left in Portugal. Wellington
had, as noted, only 38,000 with which to
oppose him, but he employed his time as

before, seeking an advantageous position of
defense where he could meet the French on
his own terms. He chose the area around the
village of Fuentes de Oñoro, just over the
border in Spain. It was nothing like as strong
a position as he had enjoyed at Busaco, but
he hoped Masséna would employ the same
unimaginative tactics as before: a simple
frontal attack.

On 3 May the marshal did precisely that,
and Wellington's infantry drove back the
attackers with the same methods employed
elsewhere in the Peninsula. A lull followed
on the 4th, but on the next day Masséna
tried again, now from the south, where he
nearly turned the allied flank.
Anglo-Portuguese troops fought stubbornly
and though pushed back, the Light Division
performed well, and the cavalry, brilliantly.
Once again Wellington's unique defensive
tactics, his close supervision of the action
and the dogged resistance of his infantry
yielded another victory, and in the end the
French withdrew. The narrow streets and
alleys were clogged with heaps of dead,
fallen in bitter hand-to-hand fighting. It was
not long before Napoleon sent the more
competent Marshal Auguste Marmont
(1774–1852) to succeed Masséna.

Wellington's victory was significant, but it
was tempered by two less fortunate events
later that week. Major-General Sir William
Erskine (1769–1813), commanding the force
investing Almeida, bungled the operation so
badly that on the night of 10/11 May, General
Antoine-Francois Brennier (1767–1832) blew
up the fortifications and managed to force his
way through the blockade with 900 of his
1,300 French troops. Wellington was livid,
declaring: 'I have never been so much
distressed by any military event as by the
escape of even a man of them.'

The Battle of Fuentes de Oñoro, 3–5 May 1811. Hoping
to relieve the besieged Portuguese border fortress of
Almeida, Masséna ordered a colossal frontal assault on
this village, which failed. A day's pause followed, and a
second attack on the third day nearly succeeded.
Wellington described his narrow victory as 'the most
difficult one I was ever concerned in and against the
greatest odds.' (Roger-Viollet)

Battle of Albuera, 16 May 1811. An extremely bloody engagement fought between an Anglo-Portuguese force under Beresford, reinforced by Spanish troops under Cuesta and Blake, and a French army under Soult that had marched north from Cadiz in order to break the Allied investment of the key fortress city of Badajoz. Beresford's mismanagement of the action cost him enormous casualties and led to his return to administrative matters. Here, Beresford grapples with and unsaddles a Polish lancer. (Engraving by Sutherland after William Heath, Philip Haythornthwaite)

For Wellington Fuentes de Oñoro put paid to a worthy adversary, but further south Marshal Soult had undertaken the conquest of Estremadura and Andalusia, in the course of which he had captured both Olivenza and Badajoz. These were solid achievements, bolstered by victory at the Gebora.

The following day, further south, Beresford had to lift his siege of Badajoz in order to prepare his defense against Soult, who with 25,000 men and 50 guns was moving up from the south to relieve the beleaguered French garrison. Beresford adopted Wellington's plan and established his 35,000 men and 38 guns around Albuera. Yet this time the French were more imaginative, and rather than a simple frontal assault, moved instead against Beresford's right, where Spanish troops, known for their unsteadiness, were positioned. The battle soon developed into a series of extremely destructive firefights fought at close range. The French might have won the day had not Sir Galbraith Lowry Cole (1772–1842), commander of the 4th Division, launched a counterattack at a critical time, obliging the French to withdraw.

The near disaster at Albuera left half of Beresford's men killed or wounded. Wellington could not contemplate a repeat of this bloodbath. Still, the battle confirmed the deserved reputation of the British soldier for receiving excessive punishment yet standing his ground: the 2nd Brigade lost 1,054 men out of 1,651, with a captain the senior surviving officer. As for Beresford, he was soon replaced by Sir Rowland Hill (1772–1842) and transferred to command the growing Portuguese army. This organizational responsibility suited Beresford far better than a field command, and he was to prove himself a great success in this role.

Albuera enabled the Allies to resume the siege of Badajoz, but when Wellington learned on 19 June that Soult and Marmont had united their armies and were marching towards the city with 58,000 men, he quickly abandoned the operation and crossed the River Guadiana. The French did not pursue – perhaps the consequence of bitter experience. By the end of the month, with Badajoz still firmly in French hands, Wellington switched his attention to Ciudad Rodrigo. Without a siege train this operation was very unlikely to succeed, and on 20 September he was obliged to withdraw when, once again, the combined forces of Soult and Marmont advanced to counter his operations. Bowing to superior numbers, Wellington raised the siege and crossed the frontier into Portugal, bringing the year's operations to a close.

Two sides to war: 'Gentlemen' and the guerrillas

The Peninsular War was a conflict of striking contradictions, for two radically different attitudes between adversaries existed side by side. Off the field of battle, and even sometimes on it, British and French troops often fraternized with one another, even to the point of dining inside each other's lines and especially to barter food, alcohol, tobacco, and clothing. Both sides occasionally arranged unofficial truces, sometimes at an individual level between rival sentries or between field commanders who wished to remove casualties from the field for medical treatment and to bury the dead. Colonel Vivian noted how 'we now ride along side by side, within five yards of each other, without any more danger of being shot than you are when hunting on the town burrows. This is doing as gentlemen should. They really are devilish civil, honourable fellows, and know how to make war …' Colonel Napier, for his part, appeared to have little reason even to dislike the French: 'I should hate to fight out of personal malice or revenge, but [have] no objection to fight for Fun and Glory.' The paradox reached truly ludicrous proportions when

one French general received through opposing lines copies of London newspapers so that he could check the fluctuating value of his investments in British government stock.

Nothing could be more further removed from this 'gentleman's war' than the nebulous but nevertheless very important 'second front' posed by the bands of guerrillas who operated against the French wherever and whenever opportunity offered itself. Although guerrilla warfare has its origins in ancient times, it was in fact the Peninsular War which made it the phenomenon familiar to us today. The Spanish word *guerrilla* means 'little war', the individual participant a *guerrillero*, which has since been revised to *guerrilla*. These were often tough, hardy men, one of whom a British soldier described as 'a swarthy, savage-looking Spaniard … armed to the teeth with pistols, daggers … a long gun, … crimson sash and free bearing, [which] at once proclaimed him as a guerrilla.'

By the very nature of their activities and loose-knit (or indeed often nonexistent) structure, guerrilla numerical strength cannot be estimated with any accuracy, as their bands could range from a handful to several thousand. What is known is that there were many separate *partidas* under numerous leaders sometimes sporting colorful nicknames such as 'El Empecinado' and 'El Medico'. While guerrilla leadership varied in character, from simple patriots to bandit leaders and even priests, their purpose, targets, and methods remained generally constant: to sever communications, cut up small detachments, ambush convoys, pick off sentries, and intercept couriers and messengers. Guerrilla numbers multiplied as the war progressed and rendered effective French rule in the provinces difficult at best and impossible at worst. In short, French authority remained in a constant state of flux, with every region unsafe to the occupier. It is no exaggeration to say that the countryside was infested. Every rock and tree became a potential place of concealment or site of ambush; every seemingly innocent peasant a possible look-out or cut-throat.

One British soldier accurately and colorfully described the guerrilla war thus:

Night and day, the French troops were not only open to attacks from the British, but in constant alarm from the natives, whose animosity made them alive to the slightest opportunity of doing them mischief. No Frenchman, however fatigued, dared to straggle or fall back because it was instant death to him. At this time the Spanish guerrillas wore their own peasant dress, not uniform, so the French could not recognise friend from foe. The guerrillas and the peasantry watched with the thirst of wolves, and slaughtered all who fell into their hands.

The countermeasures employed by the French give some idea of how effective the guerrillas were: eventually 200 cavalry would accompany a messenger to ensure safe passage, and as many as 1,000 men would escort a French general wishing to travel independently of his army. By the summer of 1813 dispatches sent by King Joseph to Paris had to be escorted by 1,500 men to guarantee safe passage to the French border.

Much of the guerrillas' ferocity was the natural consequence of French depredations, for occupying armies frequently devastated towns and villages through pillage and wanton destruction. In 1809 a British officer encountered such a place in Portugal, but the scene he describes echoes that of countless other instances occurring the length and breadth of the Peninsula:

I passed a field where the French had bivouacked. All the furniture and even the crockery had been taken from the houses of a neighbouring village and had been brought into the field. The beds and mattresses lay in rows in the mud. The drawers from the various articles of furniture had been used as mangers. Wardrobes had been transformed into bedsteads and roofs for the huts; all the crockery and glass lay in fragments on the ground. The chairs, staircases and window frames had been used partly as fuel for the kitchen fires and partly to feed huge bonfires which had been lighted when the French had withdrawn ... In the churches

Executing a monk. A not uncommon practice which did much to incense the deeply religious Spanish and increase the cycle of atrocity and counter-atrocity. Many clergy were at the forefront of encouraging resistance to the 'heretic' French, and often joined the guerrillas or fought side by side with the citizens of such cities as Saragossa and Gerona. (Goya, Roger-Viollet)

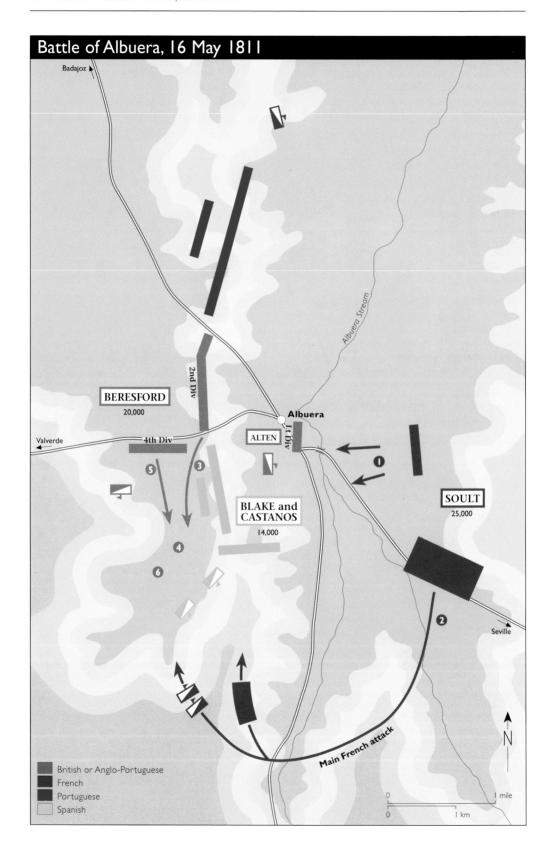

Battle of Albuera, 16 May 1811

Badajoz

Albuera Stream

BERESFORD
20,000

2nd Div

Valverde

4th Div

ALTEN

Albuera

Lt Div

1

SOULT
25,000

BLAKE and
CASTANOS
14,000

3

5

4

6

2

Seville

Main French attack

N

British or Anglo-Portuguese
French
Portuguese
Spanish

0   1 mile
0   1 km

LEFT
1. 8.00 am. French launch two feint attacks; Beresford reinforces his center.
2. 9.00 am. Main French attack with 12,000 of all arms crosses stream to threaten Spanish right flank. Spanish redeploy to face this threat and stand firm despite heavy losses.
3. 9.00 am. Part of 2nd Division moves to support Spanish.
4. 10.30 am Successful defense until sudden rainstorm prevents musket fire, leaving British infantry helpless against 3,500 cavalry. One brigade, with no time to form square, loses 1,300 out of 1,600 in a matter of minutes. Two more brigades from 2nd Division arrive to bolster defense. Storm settles; intense firefight at close range; terrible losses on both sides.
5. 4th Division (4,000 men) advances to join action.
6. 12.15 pm. French cavalry charges defeated; attacking infantry also driven off. 12.20 pm Soult commits reserve of 6,000. British attack its flanks and drive off. French retreat across river; exhaustion prevents Allied pursuit.

BELOW A French blockhouse. Built along important roads in northern Spain, these massive wooden structures housed infantry used in escorting couriers and guarding convoys. Adequate against musket fire, by 1812 they were rendered obsolete when the British supplied the guerrillas with light cannon. Ironically, at the end of the century the British themselves would be obliged to build blockhouses in order to combat their own guerrilla problem during the Boer War. (Bacler d'Albe, Roger-Viollet)

even the graves had not been spared ... Altar candlesticks ... torn vestments, chalices, prayer books and the like mixed up with straw and filth lay all about them.

Forcible requisitioning and looting by the French encouraged the peasantry to flock to the partisan bands, but it was the ill-treatment of the inhabitants themselves – documented instances of which were legion – which contributed most to fuel guerrilla activity. On entering Santarem in 1811, for instance, Rifleman Costello discovered a fountain contaminated by the mangled remains of dead Portuguese. In the town plaza he found '... murdered and violated women, shrieking and dying children. All in the village that had possessed life, lay quivering in the last agony of slaughter and awful vengeance.'

On another occasion Schaumann noted in his diary:

Never during the whole of the war did I again see such a horrible sight ... Death and destruction, murder and fire, robbery and rape

lay everywhere in the tracks of the enemy ... the burning villages, hamlets and woods ... told of the progress of the French. Murdered peasants lay in all directions.

One must not, however, discount the influence of money on those committing atrocities, for there was plunder to be acquired not merely from individual soldiers, but from their baggage wagons and convoys. One British soldier, encountering a guerrilla fresh from the kill, noted that from a silk purse he produced several human ears and fingers bearing gold rings which he claimed

Fighting guerrillas. A good impression of the type of landscape that provided ideal conditions for partisan warfare. Primitive mountain tracks, dense forests, narrow gorges, steep passes, and high cliffs left French columns, especially convoys, extremely vulnerable to ambush, sometimes by guerrilla forces large enough to annihilate forces numbering in the hundreds or even, on a few notable occasions, exceeding a thousand. (Roger-Viollet)

to have cut off from his victims in battle. 'Napoleon,' the guerrilla is reputed to have said, smiling grimly. 'Napoleon loves his soldiers, and so do the ravens. We find them plenty of food. They shall never want, so long as a Frenchman remains in Spain.'

The French for the most part found themselves unable to come to grips with such small and fluid bodies of men who fought out of uniform. The occupiers were driven to employ increasingly brutal methods in order to suppress the guerrillas, and a ferocious cycle of atrocity and counter-atrocity was begun. Outrage followed outrage as French civilian camp-followers were massacred, with villagers shot and their homes burnt in retaliation – a sharp contrast with the conduct of war in the eighteenth century, but an unmistakable foretaste of that of the twentieth. Both sides committed abominable acts of torture and murder, the French excusing their conduct on the grounds that

Guerrillas surprise and massacre a convoy of French wounded. Combatants and noncombatants alike were treated mercilessly in this ugly side of the war in the Peninsula, and even Wellington, whose operations greatly benefited from ubiquitous partisan activity, remarked that once roused a Spaniard became an 'undisciplined savage.' While guerrillas were frequently responsible for such acts of butchery as shown here, the French committed their own fair share of atrocities. (Philppoteaux; Roget-Viollet)

guerrilla violations of the normal rules of war justified all counter-measures against 'brigandage', while the partisans could hide their own repulsive measures under the guise of national liberation. In many cases, however, the guerrillas were nothing more than cut-throats intent on pillage and receiving the financial rewards offered by Wellington for intercepted French dispatches. But whatever the motives of either side, the guerrilla war rapidly became a bloodthirsty cycle of violence, costing the French an estimated 100 men a day during the course of the war and causing unquantifiable damage to the troops' morale.

French soldiers unfortunate enough to be captured by the guerrillas rarely survived the experience for long. Schaumann noted that vengeance was severe: 'The cruelties perpetrated by the Portuguese hill folk against the French soldiers who fell into their hands

are indescribable,' he observed on discovering men nailed alive to barn doors. One leader is said to have hanged every male, and disemboweled every female, prisoner. Captain François encountered 'French officers and soldiers, even women disemboweled ... Some men were put between two boards and sawed asunder ... others were buried alive up to their shoulders, or hung up by their feet over fireplaces, so that their heads burned.' There was also the grisly sight of the bodies of 400 French hospital patients, massacred after the place fell into guerrilla hands. Later he met a soldier driven insane by his experiences as the only survivor of 1,200 murdered invalids.

Some victims were stoned, others blinded with pikes, disabled and left to die in the scorching heat of the sun, or tied to trees and castrated, there left to perish from blood loss. Captain Schumacher, a cavalry trooper in the Imperial Guard, discovered the burnt remains of a military hospital set on fire with nearly 200 mutilated patients still inside. In another instance General René met an agonizing fate when his captors suspended him, feet first, over a cauldron of boiling water and lowered him by increments over the course of several hours. In short, a horrible and painful death awaited stragglers,

Surprise attack by guerrillas on a French convoy in the Salinas Pass, Navarre, 9 April 1812. One of the greatest triumphs of the celebrated leader Francisco Espoz y Mina, this exploit was nothing short of spectacular: 500 infantry of the Polish 7th Regiment, bound for Russia, were killed, 150 men were captured, 450 Spanish prisoners were released and a huge store of plunder was seized. (Philippoteaux, Roger-Viollet)

couriers, small parties of soldiers, sentries – almost anyone who fell into guerrilla hands. French retaliation, in turn, was harsh. François observed that when a party of stragglers were found tortured and murdered, the perpetrators' village was burnt while the inhabitants were lined up and shot until the guilty were identified by the next man waiting to be killed.

Operations in 1812

This year was to mark a critical point in the war, for preparations were being made by Napoleon for the invasion of Russia, a colossal undertaking which had important implications for operations in Spain, where King Joseph assumed overall command of the five French armies, totaling about 230,000 men. Napoleon's projected campaign in Russia, for which 27,000 of his

troops in the Peninsula were withdrawn, was to be waged on an unprecedented scale. Moreover, Marmont was obliged to detach 10,000 of his men to bolster the operations of Marshal Louis Suchet (1770–1826) in Valencia. Wellington now saw the opportunity he had long awaited: a general offensive into Spain. As before, this required gaining access to the northern and southern corridors, the fortresses of Ciudad Rodrigo and Badajoz, respectively. Having received intelligence of the French troop withdrawals and transfers, Wellington promptly prepared to seize Ciudad Rodrigo before the two marshals could march to its aid.

The siege began on 8 January in the depths of winter. Lieutenant Simmons recorded the hazards he encountered on the night of the 14th:

I had charge of a party to carry earth in gabions [wicker baskets] and plant them upon the advanced saps [trenches] in places where the ground was an entire rock and could not be penetrated. The enemy fired grape and consequently numbers [of men] fell to rise no more from the effects of it. I ran the gauntlet here several times and brought gabions of earth, always leaving some of my poor fellows behind when I returned for more and glad enough I was when the Engineer said 'We have now sufficient.'

Two practicable breaches were made and on the night of the 19th British troops stormed and captured the fortress at relatively low cost (500 men), but General Craufurd, the charismatic and skillful commander of the Light Division, was mortally wounded on the glacis encouraging his men in the attack. Many others died when the French exploded a mine beneath them. The troops behaved disgracefully in the aftermath, sacking the city. Simmons described a shocking practice which more than once sullied the reputation of the British Army in the wake of this and other of its bloody sieges:

… men who have stormed a town are seldom fit for anything but vice and irregularity for some time afterwards if left within its walls. The soldiers were laden with all sorts of things and looked like a moving rag-fair. Some liking their bellies better, had their swords fixed and stuck upon them large chunks of corned beef, ham, pork, etc.

Less than a week later, amid torrential rain, Wellington prepared to take Badajoz as well. He invested the place on 16 March and captured part of the outlying defenses by storm on the 24th. Without an adequate siege train Wellington's operations slowly ground on, but a sense of urgency overcame him when he learned that Soult was advancing from the south and that Marmont was moving against Ciudad Rodrigo.

Therefore, on the fateful night of 6 April, after having blasted two breaches in the bastions of Santa Maria and La Trinidad, and a third in the connecting curtain wall, a storming party was organized with the forlorn hope – a small party of men sent ahead to spearhead the main assault – led by Major O'Hare. Officers who volunteered for such perilous tasks were promised a rise in rank if they survived, and thus O'Hare's statement to a friend before setting off: 'A Lieutenant-Colonel or cold meat in a few hours.' On the signal, waves of infantry assaulted the improvised barricades placed in the breaches, put scaling ladders against the high walls of the fortress and clambered up to take the place by escalade. At least 40 attempts were made. Losses were horrendous, thousands of the besiegers falling in the storm of musketry, grapeshot, and even masonry and brick hurled down by the stalwart defenders. In the end the city was taken after a secondary attack succeeded in penetrating the rear of the town, but by the time the French surrendered allied losses had reached 5,000 men – 30 percent of the total force.

On the following morning even Wellington, known for his severe countenance, wept at the sight of so many fallen infantry. Their shock heightened by the horrendous 'butcher's bill', British troops then feasted themselves on drink and ran amok through the streets of the fallen city, defying all attempts by their officers to bring the mob under control. The French governor, Armand Philippon, and his two daughters only survived under the escort of sword-wielding British officers, while the hapless Spanish inhabitants bore the brunt of the sacking, which included numerous

British troops storm a breach at Ciudad Rodrigo, 19 January 1812. A key objective for Wellington, this fortress commanded the northern invasion route between Portugal and Spain. Major George Napier, who led one of the storming parties, recalled: 'We all mounted the breach together, the enemy pouring a heavy fire on us.' Badly wounded by grape shot, he urged his men to 'Push on with the bayonet!' – which they did, driving off the defenders. (Ian Fletcher)

British troops storming Badajoz, 6 April 1812. Costello numbered amongst those in the main assault and barely survived the experience. 'Three of the men carrying the ladder with me were shot dead in a breath … and fell upon me, so that I was drenched in blood.' This particular attack failed, but two others elsewhere eventually succeeded. Nonetheless, the combined cost of the assaults was horrific: 3,350 men, bringing the total for the siege to nearly 5,000. (Caton Woodville, National Army Museum)

dreadful instances of looting, rape and murder. The city's ordeal continued for three days before fresh troops were brought in to subdue the frenzied soldiers, and gallows were erected as a grim warning against future acts of indiscipline.

With the capture of both routes into Spain, Wellington could advance via either one, and by an offensive into central Spain he could sever communications between Marmont and Soult, endanger the French presence in Madrid and possibly take Burgos, a key point in the lines of communication back to France. Thus, detaching Hill with 18,000 to watch Soult in the south, Wellington advanced north with 48,000 men to confront Marmont, with 40,000. Wellington himself reached Salamanca on 17 June, and as neither side had a clear numerical advantage, they each sought to achieve a superior position. Several weeks of maneuvering between the rival armies followed. Many marches and countermarches were conducted in close proximity to one another, with neither side able to secure a superior position or to find a favorable opportunity to strike. At last, by late July, Wellington was ready to strike, for intelligence told him that Marmont was shortly to receive 13,000 men, sent from Madrid by King Joseph. Battle had therefore to be joined before the reinforcements arrived if Wellington was to succeed.

He chose to fight around the small village of Los Arapiles, five miles south of Salamanca, on 22 July. Both armies were marching on a parallel course about a mile apart. In the afternoon Wellington observed Marmont dangerously extending his troops over four miles and thus exposing them to defeat in detail. Wellington immediately launched an attack against the French flank, in the course of which the French were decisively defeated, losing 14,000 casualties to Wellington's 5,000. Marmont, himself wounded, retreated ignominiously and might have lost his whole force had not the Spanish, without orders, abandoned their watch over the only bridge spanning the River Tormes, thus leaving open the only possible escape route for the fugitives. Nevertheless, Salamanca was a tremendous blow to the French, and forever discredited the sobriquet 'defensive general' unfairly applied to Wellington. The battle had been won by maneuver, not merely by holding ground and repulsing the attacker. On 12 August the Allied command-in-chief entered a jubilant Madrid, where the army rested for several weeks and looked forward to regular supplies.

The next strongpoint to be attempted was the castle of Burgos, to the north of the capital. Wellington invested the place on 19 September but in the course of the following five weeks his operations suffered from woefully inadequate numbers of heavy guns and other siege equipment. Every assault launched against the defenses failed dismally and on 21 October he abandoned

the siege as French armies totaling 60,000 men converged to relieve the city. Burgos was a severe disappointment and Wellington's only major defeat of the war. The subsequent retreat, all the way back to the Spanish–Portuguese border, was a dreadful affair, like several others before it, and was conducted in appalling weather and aggravated by the loss of supplies. The march, which deprived him of nearly 10 percent of his force of 35,000 men, Wellington described as 'the worst scrape I ever was in.' At almost the same time Napoleon had left Moscow on a far more catastrophic retreat of his own. Hill was ordered to move north and Madrid was left to the French. Nevertheless, the main body eventually reached Ciudad Rodrigo on 20 November and the French pursuit had halted well before then.

Battle of Salamanca, 22 July 1812. After Vitoria, the most decisive battle of the Peninsular War, fought between Wellington and Marshal Marmont. Wellington, shown here, sought to defeat his opponent before the arrival of French reinforcements, while Marmont hoped to confront the Anglo-Portuguese army in the process of forcing it back to Portugal. Wellington caught the French in a highly vulnerable line of march, routed their forces and occupied Madrid. (AKG Berlin/British Library)

Battle of Salamanca, 22 July 1812

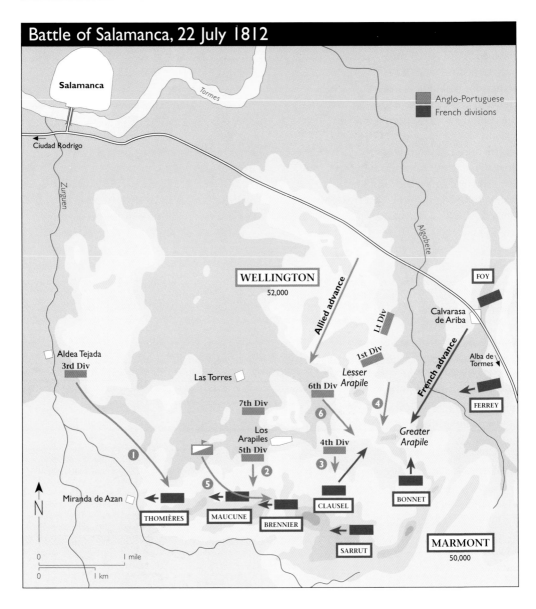

If Oporto had not convinced his detractors, Salamanca plainly demonstrated that Wellington was not merely a defensive tactician. He seized a superb opportunity for attack when a gap of about a mile opened between the two leading French divisions marching parallel to the Allied position. This weakness, and the fact that Marmont's remaining divisions were strung out for several more miles, enabled Wellington to achieve local superiority by launching a series of successful assaults throughout the day: 1) 3.30 pm. 3rd Division (7,000 men) attacks. 2) 4.15 pm. 5th Division (8,300) attacks. 3). 4.30 pm. Two brigades of 4th Division (3,900) attack. 4) 4.30 pm. Pack's Brigade (2,500) attacks. 5) 4.45 pm. 2,000 British/KGL cavalry attack. 6) 5.30 pm. 6th Division (5,500) attacks, with additional brigades in support.

Notwithstanding the failure at Burgos and the subsequent retreat, Wellington's campaign closed with some solid achievements: all French forces had been driven north of the Tagus, he had taken both vital border fortresses of Cuidad Rodrigo and Badajoz albeit at great cost in the latter case, he had severely defeated the French at Salamanca, had briefly retaken Madrid, and had captured 20,000 French prisoners and 300 guns. His army was now battle-hardened and more than confident in taking on the French, whereas French morale was low and future prospects for success had all but disappeared. Greater still for the Allies, the catastrophe which Napoleon's army had suffered in Russia not only turned the tide of the war firmly against France; for Wellington it ended all prospect of French reinforcements arriving in Spain. On the contrary, the coming campaign would actually siphon off badly needed veterans for service in central Europe. Wellington was also finally created Commander-in-Chief of the Spanish armies, totaling 160,000 men. In reality, this was more of a burden than an advantage, for they were situated across the length and breadth of the country and continued to suffer from an antiquated form of organization.

Operations in 1813

After five years on the strategic defensive, largely necessitated by the numerical superiority of the French, by 1813 Wellington was finally able to move to the offensive. Combined French forces still outnumbered those of the Allies, but the initiative had clearly passed to Wellington, and with the Russians and Prussians preparing their campaign in Germany, France would soon face a two-front war from adversaries determined to carry the conflict through to the bitter end.

In the course of the winter of 1812–13 Wellington drew up plans for the spring campaign, which were to incorporate another 5,000 men sent from home. In all, the Allied army numbered 81,000, plus 25,000 Spanish troops under Wellington's immediate control. The French, finally under King Joseph as overall commander, had 200,000 at their disposal, mostly concentrated in northern Spain and thus largely available for operations against Wellington. Wellington planned to advance north in a wide arc that would proceed around the flank of the French, who stood on the River Douro between Zamorra and Valladolid. To support this strategy Wellington planned to shift his base of supply from Lisbon to Santander, on the coast of northern Spain. In so doing he would not only

shorten his lines of communication, but place himself in a position to outflank the French well north of their present positions. To assist his operations, he organized a number of diversionary operations intended to keep French forces separated and occupied. Guerrilla operations were to be stepped up, while 18,000 men under Sir John Murray (1768–1827) would conduct an amphibious landing against Tarragona.

The new campaign season began with a rapid Allied advance in three columns which outflanked the French main defensive line and enabled Hill to take Salamanca on 26 May. The following day King Joseph fled the capital for the third time, and on 2 June Graham captured Zamorra. Caught entirely by surprise, and with their right flank continually vulnerable, the French retreated to Burgos. Wellington was not to be drawn into another costly assault, and this time he bypassed the city, obliging Joseph to retreat once again, this time to the line of the Ebro. When Graham threatened this line of defense, Joseph withdrew even further, to Vitoria, where he took up positions on 19 June. Wellington pursued closely and, in expectation that Joseph was shortly to receive reinforcements, decided to attack on the 21st.

Joseph and Jourdan, anticipating an attack, took up defensive positions with their 66,000 men near Vitoria. Expecting a straightforward assault to their front, French resistance crumbled when Wellington, with 79,000 men, assailed both flanks and pierced their center. Although some French units stubbornly held on, by 5.00 pm a rout ensued, the fugitives moving eastwards. French losses were comparatively light at 8,000, with the Allies losing 5,100, but King Joseph escaped capture by the narrowest of margins when he jumped out of one side of his coach just as a British hussar reached the other side. His army abandoned all but a handful of the 153 guns with which it had begun the battle, as well as the King's entire baggage train, including his treasury. This accounts for the failure of a vigorous pursuit, for thousands of Allied soldiers wasted several hours plundering the abandoned baggage,

Battle of Vitoria, 21 June 1813. The decisive battle of the war, it was the highlight of Wellington's bold offensive that had begun in May and culminated with Allied forces across the Pyrenees and into France herself by year's end. Anecdotes connected with the battle abound: while leading the 3rd Division in an attack on the bridge at Mendoza the fiery Sir Thomas Picton shouted to his men, 'Come on, ye rascals! Come on you fighting villains!' (German engraving, Edimedia)

making off with money and all manner of other items valued in excess of £1 million. All discipline broke down as soldiers roamed the field in search of spoil. 'In some cases,' Schaumann recalled, 'particularly over the plundering of the wagons carrying the war treasure, our men fought to the death. No officer dared to interfere. In short, more thorough and more scandalous plundering has never been known ... Our men were loaded with spoil.' At the jumble sale that followed the battle Schaumann paid bargain prices for candlesticks, teapots, silver ingots, plates and cutlery.

Although the Allied pursuit completely foundered, Vitoria proved the decisive action

of the war and the liberation of Spain now remained only a matter of time. Southern and central Spain were free of French troops, and the only garrisons remaining held the northern cities of San Sebastian and Pamplona. The wider political implications of Vitoria were great. In Germany the Russians and Prussians had arranged an armistice with Napoleon; this was broken when news of Wellington's victory reached Vienna and Austria decided to enter the struggle on the Allied side, going so far as to offer Wellington a military command in central Europe. Vitoria was, therefore, not merely decisive for the Peninsular War, but for the wider Napoleonic conflict as well.

Advancing toward the Pyrenees, Wellington appreciated that he could not undertake an invasion of southern France without first securing the border-fortresses of San Sebastian and Pamplona. He also had to consider the possible liabilities of his 25,000 Spanish troops, who were likely to pillage or worse in retribution for French atrocities committed in the Peninsula over the years. Wellington had seen the effects of guerrilla operations and did not wish to stir up a similar movement against him amongst the French populace. He therefore decided to leave behind all but a small portion of his Spanish contingent and issued stern warnings that anyone caught looting on French soil, irrespective of nationality, would meet with summary justice. Shaumann noted how, in at least one instance, General Pakenham, 'supported by a powerful guard and the provost marshal ... began to ride up and down our columns like a raving lion ... His command, "Let that scoundrel be hanged instantly!" was executed in a twinkling. Over 200 men, chiefly Spaniards and Portuguese, were put to death in this way.'

Meanwhile, Soult, re-appointed to supreme command of the remaining French forces in Spain which still numbered over 100,000 men, could still lead an offensive across the Pyrenees or maintain the advantage of defending home ground with this mountain range as a formidable – though not impenetrable – barrier. Although there were dozens of minor passes through the Pyrenees, only three routes would permit the passage of large bodies of men: the coast road at Irun, the Pass at Maya, and the Pass at Roncesvalles, all of which stood on the Spanish side of the frontier. With only 60,000 men against Soult's immediately available force of 80,000, this left Wellington to defend a front 50 miles (80 km) in length. Rather than divide his troops between the passes, he maintained a nominal force along the front and held the balance in reserve, where it could react to any French incursion. He deployed the bulk of his forces to the northeast near San Sebastian, where he believed Soult would strike first. This plan was ambitious: with limited forces he proposed to capture two fortresses while simultaneously securing the border from attack.

While Wellington busied himself deploying his troops Soult assumed command over a single army of 80,000 men which he fashioned out of the four armies (those of the North, South, Center and Portugal) which had either been withdrawn or expelled from Spain. Aware that the Allied army was overstretched and that it was expecting a French attack to relieve San Sebastian, Soult planned a counteroffensive intended to seize the passes at Maya and Roncesvalles as a prelude to the relief of Pamplona, now blockaded. Should he succeed in this, he planned to move north, defeat the Allied force besieging San Sebastian and in so doing place himself between Wellington's main force and the smaller formations elsewhere in northern Spain. Accordingly, on 25 July the French opened a surprise offensive in which General le comte d'Erlon (1774–1847), with 21,000 men, assaulted the Allied force at the pass at Maya. Despite the attackers' determined effort they faced a stout defense and the French only managed to hold the pass but not break through. On the same day, 20 miles to the south, 40,000 troops under Soult struck at Roncesvalles, seizing that strategic pass.

On hearing of the actions at Maya and Roncesvalles, Wellington made for Sorauren, 5 miles north of Pamplona, where on 27 July he took command from Cole, who had been closely pursued by the French. On the following day Soult attacked in force but was defeated, putting an end to his plans of relieving Pamplona and re-supplying his army there. Now determined on one last attempt to maintain a presence in Spain, Soult ordered three of his divisions to move west against Hill, and on 30 July d'Erlon pushed that general as far as Lizaso. On the same day, however, Wellington forced the French in the same sector to flee back to the safety of the Pyrenees. Soult had no choice but to withdraw. However, as the Allies now barred the routes through Maya and Roncesvalles, the French had to struggle north to Vera in order to make their escape. By the end of July, having suffered losses of 13,500 men from a total force of 61,000, the French stood on native soil, weakened and demoralized.

About this time, on 25 July, the Allies attempted an assault against San Sebastian. This failed, but when Graham tried again on 31 August he took the town, but not without first losing 2,300 men, followed by the castle

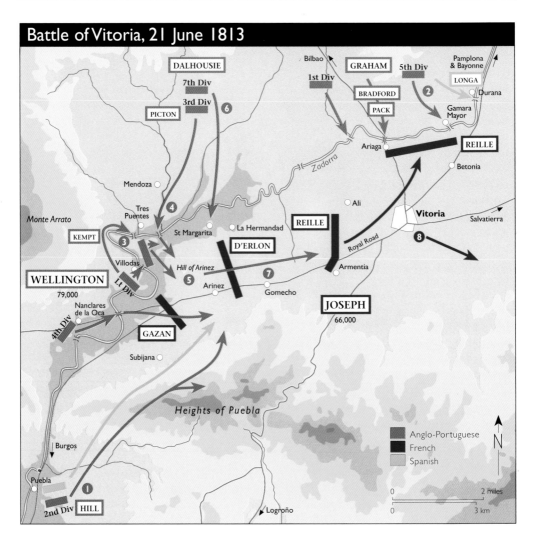

Battle of Vitoria, 21 June 1813

1. 8.00 am. Hill's corps, containing British, Portuguese, and Spanish divisions, attacks Heights of Puebla.
2. 10.00 am. Graham advances from hills and within two hours cuts French escape route along Vitoria–Bayonne road.
3. 12.00 pm. Kempt's brigade of the Light Division seizes virtually unguarded bridge at Tres Puentes.
4. 2.00 pm. Without orders, Picton's 3rd Division launches attack and seizes bridge near Mendoza.
5. 3.00 pm. Attacking from three sides, Allies capture hill and village of Arinez.
6. 3.00 pm. Dalhousie's 7th Division moves against St Margarita, but the Light Division takes it first.
7. 4.00 pm. Pressing the French on three sides, Allies advance east, breaking through.
8. 5.00 pm. French begin eastward retreat, which then dissolves into a rout.

on 7 September. As at Badajoz, the town was sacked and, perhaps unintentionally,

destroyed by fire. Also on 31 August Soult launched an attack across the Bidassoa, the river constituting the Franco–Spanish frontier to the west. His final effort to prevent an invasion of France failed when his attacks at Irun, near the coast, and at Vera, slightly inland, came to nothing. By September Austria had joined the Allied cause and French fortunes in Germany were rapidly declining.

On 7 October Wellington made his historic passage of the Bidassoa, soon crossed the mountains and entered France. The Austrians, Prussians, and Russians, meanwhile, decisively defeated Napoleon in the three-day epic Battle of Leipzig on 16–19 October, which cost the French 100,000 casualties and 100 guns and obliged the survivors to make rapidly for the Rhine.

Pamplona finally capitulated on 31 October, enabling Wellington to expand his campaign into France, all the while taking pains to treat French civilians with courtesy in order to avoid his own army being plagued by the kind of guerrilla war that had dogged the French in Spain. In fact, so scrupulous was the conduct of Allied troops that they received a better reception than did Soult's. Anyone caught looting was hanged or shot; anything acquired from the French population was paid for on the spot. Thus, with no campaign of civilian resistance to impede his progress, Wellington had little need to detach troops for static duties and could concentrate on opposing Soult.

On 10 November he overcame the marshal's strong position along the River Nivelle, forcing him to withdraw to a new defensive line along the Nive which extended from Cambo-les Bains to Bayonne and then to the Biscay coast. Wellington resumed his relentless advance on 9 December, moving on Bayonne, which he intended to invest. Yet Soult refused to abandon the initiative, and on the 10th he launched an unexpected attack near the sea against Hope, forcing him back several miles. Three days later Soult, with a 2-to-1 numerical superiority, attacked again, this time against Hill's force at St. Pierre, east of the Nive. Hill narrowly escaped a serious defeat when reinforcements appeared at a critical time, obliging Soult to withdraw. Suchet, for his part, was obliged to abandon control of Catalonia and cross the Pyrenees with his remaining force of only 15,000 men. French fortunes were now on the wane and Napoleon himself effectively admitted that the war in the Peninsula was all but lost when, in December, seeing France invaded for the first time in nearly 20 years, he wrote with disgust: 'I do not want Spain either to keep or to give away. I will have nothing more to do with that country ...' He had even greater worries to attend to personally: far to the northeast, elements of the combined armies of Russia, Prussia, Austria, and Sweden, together with numerous German allies who had finally defected from the French cause after Leipzig, had begun crossing the Rhine and were poised for a full scale invasion.

For Wellington the year had ended extremely successfully. From Portugal he had marched his army back into Spain and decisively defeated the French at Vitoria before resuming his advance northward. He had taken the last remaining fortresses, had defeated Soult in a series of actions along the Pyrenees, and had pursued his forces into France herself as far as Bayonne.

Private Edward Costello, 95th Rifles

Edward 'Ned' Costello, was born in Ireland in 1788 and joined the 95th Rifles in 1808, while a shoemaker. His battalion embarked in May 1809 for the Peninsula, where his experiences over the next five years were a series of hardships, adventures, narrow escapes, wounds, and desperate combats. Throughout his many years' of unbroken campaigning he remained a private, and his experiences, recorded for publication in 1841, provide a valuable insight into the lives of ordinary British soldiers in Wellington's army.

The 95th was a recently raised regiment, armed with the Baker rifle rather than the Brown Bess musket, and sporting distinctive dark green uniforms trimmed with black leather. 'I was highly delighted with the smart appearance of the men, and with their green uniform,' Costello wrote. The 95th (nicknamed the 'Sweeps' because of their dark appearance) not only wore different uniforms from the line regiments, their weapons provided unrivalled accuracy and their loose open-order tactics, known as skirmishing, quickly brought the 95th into prominence as an elite unit within that already distinguished element of the army, the Light Brigade, later renamed the Light Division. One of its more flamboyant riflemen was Private Tom Plunkett, who, near Astorga, had responded to General Paget's financial incentive to shoot General Colbert, who, though conspicuous on horseback, had eluded death at the hands of soldiers armed with hopelessly inaccurate smooth-bore muskets. Lying on his back in the snow and placing his foot in the sling of his weapon, Plunkett unseated the French general before running back to friendly lines, pursued by a dozen troopers.

Hardly had Costello arrived than the Light Brigade began one of history's greatest forced marches when it left to join Wellington's main body at Talavera, where a battle was shortly expected. 'Our men suffered dreadfully on the route, chiefly from excessive fatigue and the heat of the weather. The brain fever soon commenced, making fearful ravages in our ranks, and many dropped by the roadside and died.' Despite being light troops, the 95th still carried 70–80 lbs of equipment, provisions, ammunition, and a rifle, and the blistering July heat took a terrible toll. In 26 hours the Light Brigade had marched 62 miles (100 km), only to arrive at Talavera after the battle was over. But it had been an epic achievement.

As we advanced ... the heights of Talavera burst upon our sight. With three loud huzzas, we hailed the news ... The scene, however, was appalling ... The field of action ... was strewn with the wreck of recent battle. The dead and dying, thousands of them, conquerors and conquered, lay in little heaps, interspersed with dismounted guns, and shattered ammunition waggons. Broken horse trappings, blood-stained shakos [infantry helmets], and other torn paraphernalia of military pomp and distinction, completed the battle scene.

After suffering a severe fever for six weeks Costello rejoined his regiment at Barba del Puerco in March 1810. There, on the windy night of the 19th, while defending the bridge over the River Agueda over a deep chasm studded with jagged rocks, the French attacked, taking the sentries prisoner and surprising Costello and 43 other riflemen, who were on picket duty. The men sought cover in the rocky and broken ground and kept up a regular fire at those attempting to take the heights from below. Costello's company kept 600 French infantry at bay for half an hour until the colonel of the regiment brought three more companies to assist.

In July 1810, following the French capture of Ciudad Rodrigo, the French attacked the

Light Division with overwhelming numbers, in the course of which Costello and a small group of riflemen became surrounded by cavalry. 'While hotly engaged with the French infantry in our front, one or two troops of their hussars ... whipped on our left flank ... A cry of "The French cavalry are upon us" came too late, and they charged in amongst us. Taken unprepared, we could offer little or no resistance, and our men were trampled down and sabered on every side.' A French dragoon grabbed hold of Costello's collar and aimed his saber at his chest, only to be killed by a volley fired by soldiers of the 52nd Foot.

This tumbled the horse of my captor and he fell heavily, dragging me down with him. The animal was on the dragoon's leg. Determined to have one brief struggle for liberty, I freed myself from his grasp, dealt him a severe blow on the head with the butt of my rifle, and rushed up to our 52nd.

Costello, however, was shot in the right knee and while being evacuated on the back of a comrade, that man was shot, whereupon Costello dragged himself over the bridge spanning the Coa. He was lucky to have escaped with his life and this was only one of a number of similar occasions.

The retreat was typically awful, and Costello eventually reached the hospital at Belem, near Lisbon. The experiences of the sick there and at Figueira, *en route*, were quite horrendous:

The heat of the weather was intense and affected our wounds dreadfully. Doctors were scarce ... maggots were engendered in the sores, and the bandages, when withdrawn, brought away lumps of putrid flesh and maggots. Many men died on board, and others were reduced to the necessity of amputation, but by care, and syringing sweet oil into my wounds, I managed to get rid of the maggots.

With a better standard of care in Belem he soon recovered and remained to convalesce until October, when he left to rejoin his unit at the Lines of Torres Vedras.

Costello fought in numerous skirmishes and minor actions during the course of the year, pursuing the French, seeing the desolation and suffering left in their retreat, and the dreadful vengeance of the guerrillas as bodies of their victims were discovered and smoking villages marked the progress of the army. Costello fought at Fuentes de Oñoro in May 1811 and continued the advance through Spain. Like many of his comrades, he amused himself between marches and combat with wrestling and boxing matches with the peasantry, while the officers went hunting and dancing with village girls, who exchanged lessons in Spanish dance for those of England and Ireland.

At the beginning of 1812 the army laid siege to the border fortress of Ciudad Rodrigo, and when two breaches had been made in the walls Costello volunteered for the forlorn hope which was to be the small party leading in the main assault against the Lesser Breach. A second attacking party would attempt the Greater Breach. He noted that 'many of our men came forward with alacrity for this deadly service. With three officers from my company I had, as I then considered, the good fortune to be chosen. This was a momentous occasion in the life of a soldier, and so we considered it.' Shot and shell roared overhead and each man considered his chances of survival. They shook hands with each other; Costello went so far as to give his father's address to a comrade in the event he did not survive the experience. 'As darkness descended over the city,' Costello relates, 'our imaginations became awake to the horrors of the coming scene.'

'Black Bob' Craufurd, that grim but highly respected commander of the Light Division, came forward to lead the stormers in person. With a clear and distinct voice he addressed the troops:

Soldiers! The eyes of your country are upon you. Be steady, be cool, be firm in the assault. The town must be yours this night. Once masters of the wall, let your first duty be to clear the ramparts, and in doing this keep together.

Costello records that his heart beat powerfully as he and his comrades anxiously watched for the signal, while further to the rear thousands of troops of his division stood in readiness to follow up the storming party. 'We were on the brink of being dashed into eternity,' he recalled, 'and among the men there was a solemnity and silence deeper than I ever witnessed.'

On the appearance of the signal rocket Craufurd cried 'Now lads, for the breach!' and the men raced to the objective. 'As we neared the breach, the shot of the enemy swept our men away fast. Canister, grape, round-shot, and shell, with fireballs to show our ground, and a regular hailstorm of bullets, came pouring in and around us.' Craufurd fell mortally wounded, but the attack never faltered. The men scrambled up ladders placed in the ditch and ascended against a storm of fire. The attackers pushed on undaunted, though when the French sprung a mine many were killed and others scorched by the explosion. Costello himself was nearly killed by a French artillery gunner with whom he grappled until support arrived, but the whole scene was one of bitter hand-to-hand combat. In only half an hour the fight was over. The fortress was in British hands and Costello had again escaped with his life, though there were other 'scrapes' to come.

Costello would go on to participate in the even greater assault on the fortress of Badajoz in April. He again volunteered for the forlorn hope, and said of the two commanders: 'There was never a pair of uglier men, but a brace of better soldiers never stood before the muzzle of a Frenchman's gun.' Costello was wounded in the breach and 'for the first time for many years, I uttered something like a prayer.' He eventually heard the sound of firing diminish, and above the cries of the wounded he detected cheering from the town. The place had fallen, though Costello was himself wounded in the right leg, while two musket shots had perforated his helmet. Badajoz was not to be his final action, however. He would continue his march with the Light Division and go on to serve at Salamanca, the retreat from Burgos, and at Vitoria, where he took away more than £400 worth of booty from the abandoned wagons. 'All who had the opportunity were employed in reaping some personal advantage from our victory,' he wrote, 'so I determined not to be backward.' There followed the various struggles for the Pyrenees, the action at Tarbes, and finally, the Battle of Toulouse.

Costello also served in the Waterloo campaign, losing his finger to a musket ball at Quatre Bras, and for several years in the occupation of France. He spent many years again fighting in Spain during the Carlist War as part of the British Legion before becoming a yeoman warder at the Tower of London in 1838. He died in 1869, with two of the muskets balls from which he was wounded still inside him. One, which had buried itself in his leg at the Coa in 1810, was, by his request, removed after his death. In addition to his printed recollections, 'Ned' Costello can truly be said to have carried the Peninsular War with him well into the Victorian era.

The artistic works of Francisco Goya

When the French occupation began Francisco Goya (1746–1828) was 62 and already established as Spain's foremost artist. His greatest work was yet to come, inspired by the events of the next six years. Ironically this was at a time when the French would commit wholesale looting of Spanish art, from obscure pieces of statuary and painting, to native masterpieces seized from cathedrals, convents, private collections, public buildings and palaces by French officials, generals, and a host of less exalted thieves.

Even as the crisis was unfolding between Charles IV and his son Ferdinand, in the spring of 1808, Goya was engaged in an equestrian portrait of the prince for the Royal Academy of San Fernando. The picture, which was exhibited in October, was completed after only three sittings of 45 minutes each. Goya was not fond of the Spanish Royal Family and many critics agree that in earlier portraits he caricatured them, portraying them with pompous, idiotic or even cruel expressions and attitudes. The picture of the Crown

Prince was to be no exception. Ferdinand had already been deposed and Joseph Bonaparte installed in his stead, even if for the moment he and his army had been temporarily driven from Madrid.

Goya was in the capital during the fateful days of 2 and 3 May 1808 but it is not clear if he was an eyewitness to the uprising and its suppression. His records of these events, however, were left to artistic posterity in the form of two exceptionally large oils, whose vivid portrayals of the ferocity of feeling in the first instance and brutal vengeance in the second are famous around the world. The *Second of May* (*Dos de Mayo*) immortalizes one of the great moments in modern Spanish history, when residents of Madrid rose up and attacked the Mamelukes of Napoleon's Imperial Guard in the *Puerta del Sol*. The Mamelukes, men in turbans carrying curved scimitars, evoked for the *Madrileños* bitter memories of the long past but not forgotten days of Moorish occupation.

The *Third of May* shows the aftermath of the riot, as faceless French executioners dispatch suspected ringleaders and, as was perhaps inevitable in the chaos of the roundup, many innocents as well on the following evening. Goya's excellent use of color focuses the attention on a white-shirted victim with his arms raised overhead, bearing a moving expression of fatal resignation and foreboding of his imminent demise. Other victims cluster

Francisco José de Goya y Lucientes (1746–1828), c. 1815. One of Spain's greatest artists, he tackled a range of subjects and media and produced many of his most famous works during the Peninsular War. Much of Goya's art involved subtle and not so subtle parody or criticism of the Inquisition and the injustices of the state. His life was nothing if not varied and colorful, and included knife fights, womanizing, the fathering of large numbers of children, and progressive insanity. (Prado Museum/AKG Berlin)

'The Third of May, 1808' (*Tres de Mayo*). One of Goya's most famous works, depicting a French firing squad outside Madrid executing those suspected of having participated in the previous day's uprising. Although the painting is enormous – 9 feet high and 12 feet wide – in order to include both executioners and the condemned Goya placed his subjects at unnaturally close quarters, creating a peculiar perspective. It is a highly emotive, magisterial painting. (Prado, Edimedia)

around him, some already lying prostrate and slain, including one of the same figures who appears in the *Second of May* stabbing a horse. One figure cowers in the background covering his face in horror, another projects a defiant fist, while a monk in the foreground clasps his hands, probably engrossed in final prayer rather than gesturing for mercy. The colors are muted and grim – dark grays, browns, black – as opposed to the orange, red, pink, and brown used in the *Dos de Mayo*.

At the end of 1808 Goya was summoned to witness the French siege of Saragossa, near his hometown of Fuendetodos. The commander of the garrison, General Palafox, whose portrait Goya would produce in 1814, wished the artist to see the state of the city and record the heroic efforts of its citizens during that epic siege. But his journey did not result in creative work immediately, and

he returned to the capital, where throughout the remainder of the war his relationship with the French remained ambiguous. Once the occupiers returned, Goya – along with thousands of other Spaniards in state service – swore allegiance to King Joseph, and resumed his pre-war position as First Court Painter. He even accepted from the usurping king a medal, the Order of Spain, contemptuously referred to by his compatriots as 'the eggplant'.

Goya could not be properly classed a collaborator, but certainly showed no inclination towards resistance, either. In the course of the occupation he painted the *Allegory of the City of Madrid*, which represents the capital as a woman, pointing to a medallion bearing a portrait of Joseph carried aloft by figures representing Fame. Joseph's image was later replaced after his fall with the words *Dos de Mayo*, which now remain. Goya also painted several portraits of French generals and *afrancesados* (francophile Spaniards who were French sympathizers), including a fine portrait of Canon Juan Antonio Llorente, a liberal clergyman and former secretary to the Inquisition who now condemned the institution in his writings. Llorente desired social reform and saw French rule as the opportunity in which to carry it through. Goya also produced a series of pen-and-ink drawings, never actually engraved, which by their subjects sharply criticized the old injustices of the medieval Inquisition. Other sketches, which too remained only on paper and were never reproduced as engravings, portrayed thousands of nuns and monks, removed from their religious houses by French edict, engaging in the human pleasures hitherto denied them by their strict vows. His superb portrait of 1810 of Nicholas Guye, a distinguished French general, so impressed the sitter that Guye commissioned a picture of his young nephew as well.

But Goya also painted the liberator as well as the occupiers, and when the French evacuated the Spanish capital in 1812 the grateful *Madrileños* provided a rapturous welcome to Wellington, who soon commissioned an equestrian portrait of himself, followed later by two other portraits. None of these betray a heroic figure; rather a somewhat wearied one. The equestrian portrait shows him in a blue Spanish cavalry cloak, covering the otherwise striking scarlet uniform of the British Army; he has a somewhat undersized head, and rides alone in a bleak landscape – quite in contrast to David's heroic portrayal of *Napoleon crossing the Alps* (1800). The half-length portrait of the Duke is recognized as an accurate likeness but is certainly not meant to evoke images of grandeur as was clearly the case in the full-length portrait of him later executed by Sir Thomas Lawrence. He does indeed wear his uniform, replete with his various decorations and medals from Britain, Portugal, and Spain, yet neither his pose nor his expression evoke the kind of passion so common amongst other military portraits of the neoclassical age.

Goya did not confine himself only to the famous; in the course of the war he painted family portraits and pictures of various private individuals. Indeed, the subjects of his wartime work varied greatly. Many of his portraits exude quiet simplicity, gentleness, and even beauty. He painted his son's mother-in-law and father-in-law; his grandson; three children of noted Madrid

families; a well-known actress named Antonia Zárate; and the attractive Francisca Sabasa García. In addition to portraits he produced works showing ordinary scenes of life and work in numerous paintings such as *The Water Carrier*, *The Knife Sharpener*, and *The Forge*, an image of blacksmiths at work. Goya continued the theme of earlier prewar subjects, like the *majas* – alluring young women in provocative poses. In contrast, other women appear in *Old Age* and *Celestina and her Daughter*, works which illustrate the irreversible ravages of time on human beauty.

Without doubt Goya's best known work at this time focused on the war. There was the forbidding and inscrutable *Colossus* (c. 1811, Museo del Prado). This naked giant, possibly symbolizing war, strides across the landscape towering above throngs of terrified refugees and their herds as they flee in all directions in a scene of total chaos. The most notable of his wartime work revealed a very different side to the portrayal of the conflict itself and was the antithesis of the glorious battle scenes created by the likes of Jacques-Louis David (1748–1825) and Antoine Gros (1771–1835). Goya's images are patently not about heroes and victories. His series of 82 etchings entitled the *Disasters of War* (*Desastres de la Guerra*), originally drawn in red crayon, which were executed throughout the war though not published until 1863, represent a stark and haunting record of the conflict and his unequivocal views upon it. The modern iconography of war may be traced from them, as can the tradition of the artistic witness to conflict. These powerfully haunting etchings reveal the baseness to which human nature can descend when the extremities of war bring out his more barbarous instincts. Yet they constitute more than a condemnation of the horrors of the war in the Peninsula, for they also record numerous instances of injustice, oppression and hypocrisy on the part of Spanish officials and clergy.

But the brutality of war emerges above others as the dominant theme. Some have allegorical references – some subtle and others flagrantly transparent – drawing the observer's attention to the viciousness of war and its dire influence on society, religion, and human behavior. There is symbolic use of animals: wolves, pigs, eagles, donkeys, and others, each representing something sinister, stupid or ignorant. Most are straightforward in their ghastliness, depicting the worst excesses of conflict: rape, massacre, pillage, torture, homelessness, starvation. Individuals in the *Disasters*, whether the perpetrator of some outrage or its victim, are sometimes rendered almost nonhuman, while in contrast the humanity of others is unquestionable. Goya's art of this period illustrates a living hell: a hell wrought from war and its attendant miseries. Tradition states that when Goya's servant asked him why he produced such dreadful scenes of man's inhumanity to man, the artist replied, 'To tell men forever that they should not be barbarians.'

The *Disasters* remained unpublished for 35 years after Goya's death; they were clearly not meant as propaganda and their publication would certainly have led to his arrest by French authorities. On the other hand, even at the restoration of Ferdinand Goya did not see fit to release them, undoubtedly because of the offence they would have caused to a monarch who, having cravenly first colluded with Napoleon in ousting his father and then abdicated in favor of a Bonaparte king, bore a

French depredations. An engraving from Goya's *Disasters of War*, showing French soldiers abusing Spanish women. Faceless figures cower in the shadows and a baby lies crying on the floor. Rape was an all too common feature of this ghastly conflict. (Museum of Fine Arts, Boston/Roger-Viollet)

heavy responsibility for the occupation. Ferdinand had played no part in the war of independence, notwithstanding which its victims focused their hopes on his return from exile.

The *Disasters* may be divided into three main themes, the first of which shows the reaction of rural Spaniards to the invasion. Bodies heaped together, peasants fighting with improvised weapons against the invader, executions and murder all find their place here. A second theme concentrates on urban life, with its squalor and starvation, doubtless inspired by the terrible famine that struck Madrid in 1811–1812. The last theme is more political in tone, revealing how with the close of the war and the restoration of the monarchy under Ferdinand VII, whose reign would continue until 1833, a new phase of cataclysm afflicted the nation.

The first etching in the series depicts a man kneeling, arms outstretched and eyes beckoning the heavens as if desperately seeking an answer for the misfortunes that have befallen him. 'Gloomy presentiments of things to come' reads the caption. Goya did not shrink from scenes of horror; instead, he recorded them bleakly, whether it was mutilated corpses, starving civilians or the wanton excesses of French troops. What emerges is an indictment of man's inhumanity to man, observed by an eyewitness to the atrocities he depicts.

Evidence of such atrocities is supported by the written records of others: Spaniards, French, and British. Simmons of the 95th witnessed the desolation of a Portuguese town in 1811:

… the houses are torn and dilapidated, and the few miserable inhabitants moving skeletons; the streets strewn with every description of household furniture, half burnt and destroyed, and many streets quite impassable with filth and rubbish, with an occasional man, mule or donkey rotting and corrupting and filling the air with pestilential vapours … Two young ladies had been brutally violated in a house that I entered and were unable to rise from a mattress of straw. On the line of march, comparing notes

*with other officers, I found that they all had
some mournful story to relate of the savage
French vandals which had come under their
immediate observation … The unfortunate
inhabitants that have remained in their villages
have the appearance of people who have been
kicked out of their graves and reanimated.*

Some plates show refugees, huddled
together, emaciated, dejected, reduced to
begging. Other etchings show dismembered
corpses impaled on the branches of trees.
Again, such scenes are corroborated by others,
no less than Wellington himself: 'I have seen
many persons hanging in the trees by the
sides of the road,' he wrote, 'executed for no
reason that I could learn, excepting that they
had not been friendly to the French
invasion … the route of their column on their
retreat could be traced by the smoke of the
villages to which they set fire.'

Such scenes inspired Goya's *Disasters*. In
his twenty-ninth etching, entitled, 'They do
not want to', a French soldier clutches the
waist of a Spanish woman who in her
struggle claws at her assailant's face while an
elderly woman, presumably the mother,
stands behind the soldier brandishing a
dagger to be plunged into his back. Other
etchings show naked corpses of civilians
grotesquely strewn on the ground, as
onlookers cover their faces in horror. Still
others show monks dispossessed of their
monasteries, and a sinister depiction of a
wolf, sitting amongst a group of emaciated
and dejected peasants, scribbling in quill pen
on a parchment condemning the suffering
and misery of the war. 'Wretched humanity,'
the caption reads, 'the fault is yours.'

The etchings that comprise the *Disasters of
War* together reveal how Goya was revolted
by war with its destruction of the nation's
spirituality, the brutalization of people
driven to reprisal against the invader,
ceaseless destruction and bloodshed, and the
privations of ordinary noncombatants,
victims of a war they neither inspired nor
perpetuated. Nevertheless, Goya did not
confine his subject to atrocities and privation
alone; some of his etchings clearly condemn

Atrocities. One of the many eyewitness sketches by
Goya in his series *The Disasters of War.* Far from
romanticizing war like so many of his predecessors and
contemporaries, Goya depicted the more gruesome,
barbaric sides of the Franco-Spanish element of the
conflict. Here he depicts mutilated corpses suspended
from a tree – a not uncommon sight recorded by many
other observers. (Museum of Fine Arts,
Boston/Roger-Viollet)

the betrayal of liberal political reforms
instituted by the Cortes during the war. In
'Truth is dead', the artist shows figures
representing the return of repressive
institutions to Spain standing over the
corpse of a young woman representing
Truth. Her body emanates light while the
clergyman presiding over her funeral appears
dark and foreboding. Before the corpse
kneels the figure of Justice covering her face
with her hands in abject sorrow. Such
political themes symbolized a particularly
painful expression of hopes unfulfilled in the
wake of liberation. Ordinary Spaniards, who
had exalted the cause of Ferdinand, casting
him as something of a savior, soon lost their
fervor when the restoration reestablished the
Old Order with a vengeance. No sooner had
Ferdinand returned to Spain than he
abrogated the Constitution of 1812 and
executed the leaders of the Cortes. Such
repression ill repaid the Spanish people for
the experience of six years of misery and
Goya was not loath to record it.

George Canning, British Foreign Secretary, 1807–1809

'I hope,' announced George Canning (1770–1827), in a speech he gave near the end of his long political career, 'that I have as friendly a disposition towards the nations of the earth, as anyone who vaunts his philanthropy most highly; but I am contented to confess, that in the conduct of political affairs, the grand object of my contemplation is the interest of England.' This was particularly the case in the realm of foreign affairs and when he became Foreign Secretary in the Duke of Portland's government in March 1807, Canning's principal aims lay in preserving Britain's existing alliances and at the same time seeking to establish others.

Canning assumed office while British fortunes were at one of their lowest points since the start of the Napoleonic Wars four years earlier. His primary responsibility, that of maintaining the Anglo-Russian alliance, proved all but impossible, for Napoleon had already severely checked the Tsar's army at the Battle of Eylau in February, and in June the French victory at Friedland and the peace of Tilsit knocked Russia out of the war altogether, leaving Britain with no allies apart from feeble Sweden and Portugal.

By a secret clause of the treaty Russia agreed that if Denmark should fail to close its ports in accordance with the Continental System, it would support French hostility against Denmark. When Canning learned through covert means of French intentions, he persuaded the cabinet to send a fleet to demand the surrender of the Danish fleet for the duration of the war, thus anticipating Napoleon's plans. As a neutral power, Denmark naturally objected to the British ultimatum. In September Copenhagen was ruthlessly bombarded and occupied and the Danish fleet carried away. The legality of the operation was certainly questionable, but

Canning recognized that with the Danish fleet, together with that of Portugal, in French hands, Napoleon could once again threaten Britain with invasion. Decisive though Trafalgar had been two years before, Britain's security from attack remained foremost in the minds of policy-makers in London.

The following month Canning successfully arranged the hand-over of the Portuguese fleet to the Royal Navy. As has been shown, Admiral Sir Sidney Smith appeared before Lisbon at the end of October, evacuated the royal family and escorted it and the Portuguese fleet to Brazil, just as Junot was approaching the undefended capital. Thus, within the space of a few months, Napoleon had been denied the ships which he would require if he was to threaten Britain directly – thanks in great measure to Canning's foresight and boldness.

Successful as this defensive strategy had proved, it was now time for more active measures. Britain needed a foothold on the Continent – a place from which her albeit limited military resources could be brought to bear in a major and sustained land campaign. That prospect did not arise, as has been shown, until the Spanish rose in spontaneous revolt, and when on 8 June 1808 emissaries from Asturias arrived in London seeking British aid, it was Canning, in his capacity as Foreign Secretary, to whom they applied. When the deputies were soon followed by their counterparts from Galicia and Andalusia, all seeking money and arms, Canning saw a golden opportunity to strike another blow against France, this time through the active resistance of patriots eager to fight.

In Canning's view a war of national resistance had much to recommend itself. As early as 1795 Britain had witnessed with bitterness her monarchical allies detach

George Canning. Working tirelessly to maintain harmonious Anglo-Spanish relations came with its share of obstacles. 'At present,' he wrote in August 1809, 'the Spanish think they are sure of us; and that they have a right to us; and that instead of every assistance that we afford them being another matter of fresh acknowledgement, every point upon which we hesitate is an injury, and a breach of engagement. This tone of theirs is offensive, and becomes irksome to me.' (Roger-Viollet)

He has fought against countries in which the people have been indifferent to his success; he has yet to learn what it is to fight against a country in which the people are animated with one spirit to resist him.

Canning himself declared that the government would furnish whatever practical support it could, notwithstanding the fact that, officially, Britain and Spain remained in a state of war. 'We shall proceed,' he told the House in one of the many masterful speeches of his parliamentary career,

upon the principle that any nation of Europe that starts up with a determination to oppose a Power which, whether professing insidious peace, or declaring open war, is the common enemy of all nations, whatever may be the existing political relations of that nation with Great Britain, becomes instantly our essential ally.

In short, hostilities with Spain would immediately cease and, most significantly, Britain would assist any nation or people prepared to oppose Napoleonic aggression.

Canning backed his words with material assistance: he immediately arranged a treaty of peace between Britain and Spain and appointed a diplomatic representative to the juntas. On 5 August he responded to the practical wants of the same, asking Lord Castlereagh (1769–1822), who went on to serve as an acclaimed Foreign Secretary but was then the Secretary of State for War, for artillery and cavalry on behalf of the Asturian and Galician deputies. He made several requests to Lord Chatham at the Board of Ordnance for supplies of weapons, and by November 160,000 muskets had been

themselves one by one from their respective alliances in violation of treaties which had uniformly prohibited all signatories from concluding a separate peace. Canning had, moreover, seen every attempt to support the minor powers of Europe with troops or aid, such as to Hanover, Denmark, Sweden, Portugal, and Naples, fail dismally. The nature of the conflict in the Peninsula, on the other hand, was singular and unprecedented. A popular rising led by people prepared to die for their country rather than merely a king seemed to offer a much greater hope of success in the long struggle against Napoleonic hegemony.

On 15 June Richard Sheridan, a friend and parliamentary colleague of Canning, brought the question of aid to the House of Commons. In the past, he observed,

Bonaparte has had to contend against princes without dignity and ministers without wisdom.

sent, with 30 to 40,000 more to follow within the next month. Spanish demands for money were considerable and initially exceeded the British government's ability to meet them, but within a month of the deputies' arrival a diplomat had been dispatched to Corunna with £200,000 in Spanish dollars for the Galician junta. By summer's end the five main juntas between them had received over £1,000,000 in silver and more would be available to the Supreme Junta on its formation.

Canning appreciated that his nation's contribution must extend beyond the mere provision of finance and supply: Britain must send an army of its own. Circumstances were more favorable now than ever before, for with the invasion threat relieved by the neutralization of the Danish and Portuguese fleets Britain no longer required a large concentration of troops for home defense. Canning therefore strongly advocated plans to release some of these for service abroad and, as has been shown, in early June Wellesley embarked for the Peninsula with an expedition in support of the Spanish (and Portuguese) which, ironically, had been intended for operations against Spanish America.

The initial results have already been discussed: in August Wellesley landed in Portugal and soon defeated Junot at Vimiero. Sir Arthur might have pursued and destroyed the French entirely, had not his superiors, Generals Dalrymple and Burrard, first prevented him, and then concluded the infamous Convention of Cintra, which arranged for the evacuation of Junot's army back to France in British ships. It took 11 days for official word to arrive in London and on the 16th the terms of Cintra appeared in the newspapers with predictable results. Public opinion, at a pitch of enthusiasm for the war in the Peninsula, began to subside at the news that the hitherto invincible French, having been defeated in the field, would be evacuated home, complete with arms and booty and free to fight again.

Canning was livid, describing the convention to Chatham as 'both disgraceful

and disastrous in the highest degree.' To Lord Bathurst he called it 'so utterly, manifestly, shamefully unjust, that I hope and believe the Portuguese people will rise against it.' To allow the French to retain plunder seized from Britain's ally was nothing short of scandalous, and the act would thereafter remain 'as a sort of landmark for the guidance of future commanders, a terror to our allies, and an encouragement to our enemies.' Despite Canning's vehement objections the cabinet reluctantly conceded that the convention must be honored, though the Foreign Secretary did secure the recall of Dalrymple, Burrard, and Wellesley, the first two of whom were denied any further opportunity for active service.

If Cintra were not enough, the second blow to British arms, Sir John Moore's retreat to Corunna, also infuriated Canning, who both condemned the general for 'running away' and blasted the Spanish for failing to support him with provisions and information on French dispositions. Even before Moore had made the decision to retreat to northwest Spain rather than to Portugal, Canning was determined that Spanish authorities not construe this as a general British policy of abandonment. The army would definitely return, he wrote on 9 December to the British representative to the Supreme Junta, but when it was able to do so it must have the supplies and intelligence it rightfully required from Spanish officials. It was not, the Foreign Secretary insisted, to be divided up among the different Spanish armies, but must remain unified under British commanders and left to conduct itself according to plans conceived by officers in the field under orders from the government in London.

The British Army, Canning continued, 'will decline no difficulty, it will shrink from no danger, when through that difficulty and danger the commander is enabled to see his way to some definite purpose.' He rebuked the Spanish for the shortcomings of which Moore had complained in his dispatches. In short, the army must never in future be

Sir John Moore being carried from the field of Corunna. Mortally wounded after being struck by a round shot on the left shoulder, he died later that night, mourned by an army whose respect for him often extended to adoration. Sir George Napier reflected popular sentiment when he described the fallen general as ' ... a model for everything that marks the obedient soldier; the persevering, firm and skilful general; the inflexible and the real patriot ...' (Ann Ronan Picture Library)

abandoned 'in the heart of Spain without one word of information, except such as they [Moore and Baird] could pick up from common rumour, of the events passing around them.' Before Moore could be expected to return in support of his allies, the Spanish must offer a full explanation of their strategy.

During the closing days of December Canning privately condemned Moore's failed campaign in increasingly stronger terms, but his cabinet colleagues did not share his opinion. With the arrival of news of the successful evacuation of the army and of Sir John's death in action, the Portland ministry chose instead openly to endorse the conduct of an otherwise popular general who had saved the army from certain doom at the cost of his own life.

The time for the government to defend its policy in Parliament was not long in coming, and at the end of February 1809 the Opposition duly moved a motion demanding an enquiry into 'the causes, conduct and events of the last [campaign] in Spain.' Inevitably, they attacked the government for both Cintra and Corunna. Canning, privately exasperated but loyal to Portland, replied, giving what one of his colleagues described to the King as 'one of the best, most eloquent and commanding speeches that was ever heard.' Moore, he declared, had played an instrumental part in disrupting Napoleon's declared object of destroying Spanish opposition in the field once and for all. Indeed, the advance as far as Sahagun, the Foreign Secretary declared, was nothing less than the work of a statesman, not merely that of a soldier.

Canning strenuously maintained that the Spanish will to resist had thus remained intact, and, in the great British tradition of characterizing defeat as victory, insisted that although Moore's army had been pushed out of Spain, his triumph at the Battle of Corunna had left 'fresh laurels blooming upon our brows.' He condemned those who conceded defeat and counseled withdrawal from the Peninsula (British forces still remained in Portugal, of course), and insisted that Napoleon could ultimately be overcome. Closing his oratory, Canning acknowledged that Napoleon's fortunes had doubtless been improved by recent events, 'but still it was fortune, not fate; and therefore not to be considered unchangeable and fixed.'

The discrepancy between Canning's private opinions about Moore's conduct and his public statements on the subject seems hypocritical. However, the situation was complex, for if the ragged troops who disembarked on the south coast of England were to be believed, the Spanish had severely let them down. There were stories of Spanish cowardice in the field – a charge not always justified – as well as indifference to the plight of British troops retreating in the face of overwhelming French forces. To this were added shocking revelations about the Spaniards' failure to provide food and shelter to Moore's desperate men. Thus armed, many on the Opposition benches in Parliament argued that a third attempt to stop the French in the Peninsula was hopeless. Canning disagreed, and while he privately decried the incompetence of Spanish generals and the Supreme Junta, he continued to maintain both in public and private that Britain ought to support the patriotic cause of the Spanish people with all practical means. The government won the debate, public fears were assuaged, and Britain would carry on its commitment to the war in the Peninsula.

In his task of securing and sustaining Spain as a vital ally, Canning had difficulties beyond Parliamentary opposition. Spanish and Portuguese requests for arms and money were incessant, prompting the Foreign Secretary to complain to a friend in July 1809 that in the course of the war with France 'we have supplied by turns almost the whole continent with arms – Russia, Prussia, Sweden, Portugal, Sicily and Spain – while at the same time our own military establishments are sixfold what they formally were ...' When the Portland ministry resigned in September, Canning had not managed to conclude a definitive Anglo-Spanish treaty of alliance establishing mutual responsibilities and benefits. Still, in the end, common hostility to France continued to keep two otherwise traditional enemies on a fairly steady, if at times rocky, course and a formal treaty of alliance shortly followed.

Canning's brief tenure as Foreign Secretary under Portland had – at least respecting the war in the Peninsula – borne considerable fruit. Anglo-Spanish relations had swiftly turned from hostility to friendship under Canning's direction, while Britain's provision of the three elements so essential to the success of the conflict – troops, weapons, and money – owed much to Canning's strong advocacy of the Spanish cause. Although he left office well before the end of the Peninsular War, Canning's connection with foreign affairs generally, and with Spain in particular, was by no means over. In 1822 he returned for a lengthy stay at the Foreign Office, where his attention was devoted to such critical international issues of the day as Spain's political crises, and the problem of French intervention in them, the future of the Congress System and Britain's role in it, the complex issue of Greek independence, and the recognition of, and establishment of trade with, the newly independent states of Latin America. His exceptionally deft handling of these and other thorny issues would eventually establish Canning as one of Britain's greatest foreign secretaries.

Anti-climax: The campaign of 1814

At the opening of the campaign Wellington had 63,000 men, plus his Spanish troops, at his disposal. With these forces he intended to divide the French by drawing Soult away from Bayonne. He would achieve this by maneuvering around the French flanks, a strategy that had succeeded admirably the previous year. Soult had 54,500 men, having been stripped of 10,000 men and 35 guns by the Emperor in the first month of the year. These forces were divided approximately equally between those defending Bayonne, just above the River Adour, and those along the Joyeuse, about 10 miles east of the Nive, in Allied possession since December.

With his 31,000 men Hope began to besiege Bayonne, with orders to pass the Adour as opportunity allowed. While Wellington held back four divisions in reserve at the Nive, Hill moved eastwards with 13,000 men, crossed the Joyeuse on 14 February and three days later reached St Jean-Pied-de-Port. Soult responded by drawing off two divisions from Bayonne, leaving it with only 17,000 men. It was for just such a weakening of defenses that Wellington had hoped. Hope crossed the Adour west of the city on the 23rd by boat and established a lodgement on the opposite bank. Then, having constructed a bridge across the river, by the 26th he had 15,000 men on the other side, leaving Bayonne encircled and cut off from the remainder of Soult's forces.

The French had retreated before Hill's advance with 13,000 men as far as Orthez:

Wellington now opposed them with 31,000 men. At Orthez Soult established his 36,000 men and 48 guns on a ridge west of the city – a strong defensive position. On 27 February Wellington's first assault failed, but his second, now supported from the east by a separate attack by Hill, succeeded, and Soult withdrew in order to save his army from being trapped in the city. A fortnight later, on 12 March, Bordeaux, having declared its support for the Bourbon throne, opened its gates to Beresford. Soult meanwhile continued his withdrawal, his rearguard fighting with spirit at Tarbes on 20 March. Four days later he entered

Lieutenant-General Sir Rowland Hill, 1st Viscount Hill (1772–1842). Arguably Wellington's best subordinate commander, Hill proved himself able in independent command through his victory at Arroyo dos Molinos in 1811, but also in every action in which he served, particularly Vitoria, the Nivelle and the Nive. His scrupulous attention to his own troops' welfare and material needs earned him the nickname 'Daddy Hill'. (Stipple engraving, 1815, Ann Ronan Picture Library)

Major-General William Beresford, Viscount Beresford (1768–1854). He led a division under Wellesley and Moore before his appointment in 1809 as Marshal of the Portuguese army, which was then in a pitiful state. Beresford showed exceptional skill at reorganizing and training the Portuguese, whose language he learned, and through his reforms and the integration of British officers into their ranks he created a respectable fighting force which played an important role in ultimate victory. (Ann Ronan Picture Library)

RIGHT
1. 5.00 am. Hill demonstrates on west bank of Garonne toward suburb of St Cyprien.
2. 5.00 am. Picton, ordered to make feint attack, disobeys and opens all-out assault; repulsed with heavy casualties.
3. Beresford, with two divisions, marches between Calvinet Ridge and River Ers in preparation for main attack against southern section of the ridge. Advance seriously delayed by mud and swampy banks of Ers.
4. Freire, mistakenly believing Beresford in his designated position and attacking, strikes north end of Calvinet Ridge with two Spanish divisions as planned; badly repulsed.
5. Beresford opens attack against Sypière Redoubt; French counterattack of two brigades repulsed. Beresford renews attack against spirited opposition.
6. 2.00 pm. Picton renews his attack, with Spanish support, but with few gains. Beresford attacks again; redoubt taken and retaken five times in savage struggle for possession.
7. 5.00 pm. French begin withdrawal from Calvinet Ridge into city.

with an assault against Toulouse, where Soult had 42,000 men entrenched on a ridge to the east of the city, itself protected by the Garonne to the west and the Ers to the east. Beresford moved with two divisions against the southern end of the ridge, while diversionary attacks were launched from the north and west. After 12 hours of fierce fighting, in which the Spanish, at first repulsed, then returned with success, the French were driven back, and evacuated the city the following day. On the 12th Wellington found the theater decorated with laurel by the residents, who cheered the conqueror's entry as a band played 'God save the King'. The same evening Wellington learned of Napoleon's abdication. Soult thought the report false and was therefore not prepared to capitulate, but accepted Wellington's offer of an armistice.

News of the fall of Napoleon had not yet reached Bayonne, which remained besieged by Sir John Hope. On the night of the 14th General Thouvenot made a desperate sortie from the city in a gamble to break the Allied stranglehold. He failed, and in the attempt each side suffered about 800 casualties. On the 17th Soult, having received confirmation on the 12th that the abdication was genuine, finally surrendered. Bayonne followed suit

Toulouse, where it was possible Suchet might join him by fighting his way north.

Ten days later, on 30 March, the Allied armies to the north captured Paris and on 6 April Napoleon abdicated unconditionally. However, news of this would take some time to reach Soult and Wellington, and in the meantime the latter hoped to prevent the possibility of any junction between Soult and Suchet. He therefore struck first, on 10 April,

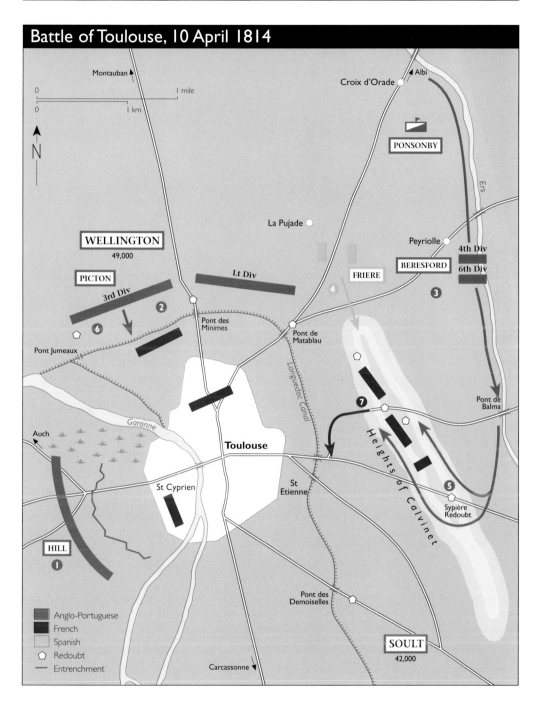

Battle of Toulouse, 10 April 1814

Montauban

0 ——————————————— 1 mile
0 ——————————————— 1 km

N

Croix d'Orade   Albi

PONSONBY

Ers

La Pujade

WELLINGTON
49,000

Peyriolle   4th Div

PICTON   Lt Div   FRIERE   BERESFORD   6th Div

3rd Div   4   3

②

⑥

Pont des
Minimes

Pont Jumeaux   Pont de
Matablau

Pont de
Balma

Garonne

Languedoc Canal

Auch

Toulouse   ⑦

St Cyprien   St
Etienne   Heights of Calvinet

⑤

Sypière
Redoubt

HILL

①

Pont des
Demoiselles

SOULT
42,000

Anglo-Portuguese
French
Spanish
◇ Redoubt
— Entrenchment

Carcassonne

on the 26th. After more than six years, and
for reasons external to the immediate
conflict, the Peninsular War was finally over.

In the immediate aftermath of the
conflict Wellington was appointed British
Ambassador to France. His army was broken
up: some regiments returned home, others

were disbanded, while still others
disembarked at Bordeaux for service against
the United States, with whom Britain had
been at war since June 1812.

However important a role the Peninsular
War played in the defeat of France, it is
important to recognize that the war did not

end as a result of a decisive battle in the style of Austerlitz, Jena or Friedland. On the contrary, when the Allied armies occupied Paris and obliged Napoleon to abdicate, resistance in the south of France, though failing, was still very much under way. Thus, although Wellington's campaign in 1814 did not directly lead to French surrender, it nevertheless contributed to it by occupying Soult in the south.

Battle of Toulouse, 10 April 1814. The last major action of the Peninsular War, it was fought, unbeknownst to both sides, four days after Napoleon had unconditionally abdicated. Driven from most of his outer defenses after bitter fighting, Soult withdrew inside the city walls, only to realize that once Allied artillery was dragged up the heights his occupation would become untenable. The French therefore retreated south on the evening of the 11th. (Engraving by A. Dupray, Philip Haythornthwaite)

Losses, lessons and legacy

Impact on Spain and Portugal

The physical devastation wrought by the war was immense, particularly in Spain, where years of occupation had brought comprehensive requisitioning, pillage, and just plain mayhem, not to mention the destruction wrought by the fighting. After the war Spain entered a period of tyranny and political instability. This was not the result of a hardening of political attitudes or the growth of a strain of arch-conservatism produced in reaction to the liberalism of the Bonapartist regime in Madrid; rather it was a reaction to internal reforms undertaken by what amounted to a regency government. While the regional juntas and the Church had been busy waging their war against the 'heretics' from the north, the Cortes, which had spent most of the war shut up in besieged Cadiz, had functioned on broadly liberal principles. In 1812 this body produced a constitution that guaranteed limited forms of political and religious freedom, reforms which were unprecedented. With high hopes the Cortes established a regency council in early 1814 in anticipation of the imminent return of Ferdinand VII. Their expectation rested on the King swearing allegiance to the new constitution and accepting the limitations that it imposed on his rule.

These hopes were quickly dashed; although he had accepted the Constitution of 1812 before he left captivity, Ferdinand returned from exile on 24 March 1814 and immediately took repressive measures against the liberals. On 22 April 69 deputies to the Cortes denounced the liberals and the Constitution of 1812 in their *Manifesto de las Persas*. This was swiftly followed by the repudiation of the Constitution by

Ferdinand himself on 4 May. Six days later the liberal leaders in Madrid were arrested. Ferdinand's repressive methods and political ineptness proved so unpopular that they led to an attempted military coup in Pamplona in September, led by the former guerrilla leader, Francisco Espoz y Mina. The revolt involved army officers, angered by the King's favoritism toward nobles who had had no part in the war, as well as lower ranks whose disaffection sprang from unpaid wages and the likelihood that they would have to serve in the Americas to quell the colonial rebellions there. The coup was suppressed, but others, also unsuccessful, followed in September 1815 in Corunna, and in April 1817 in Catalonia.

In July 1819 Major Rafael Riego led a failed military conspiracy in Cadiz, but by early the following year, after he had announced his support for the Constitution of 1812, the military revolt began to spread throughout the country, forcing Ferdinand to accept the Constitution and appoint a new government on 7 March 1820. The new Cortes assembled in Madrid in July and at the end of August Riego entered the capital a popular hero. Yet the story of political instability did not end here, for a series of short-term ministries and army revolts followed until France – now of course Bourbon – sent an army into Spain in April 1823 in order to restore order and return Ferdinand to complete control over his troubled country. More revolts and the Carlist War followed. Thus, the end of French occupation and the bitter conflict that it had inspired only set the scene for two decades of further misery and bloodshed. Nevertheless, the generation following the French invasion saw the dismantling of the legal structure of the Old Regime and many of the privileges of the old establishment were removed. The Church was stripped of most of its land and a new class of landowner emerged. Spain did not become a democracy, but after 1834 it had embraced a number of principles of political liberalism.

The war also dramatically affected the Spanish Empire. A rebellion broke out in Mexico in September 1810, and Venezuela declared its independence in July 1811, beginning more than 10 years of conflict between royalists and nationalists led by Simón Bolívar. Most of Spain's New World Empire became independent in the decade following these revolts.

In Portugal, John VI succeeded as King on the death of his mother in March 1816, but he did not return from Brazil until 1821. The fact that the Portuguese royal family had taken refuge in Brazil helped account for that

Simón Bolívar (1783–1830), the 'Liberator' of South America. Bolívar fought in the unsuccessful Venezuelan revolt of 1811–1812, and in New Granada (Colombia) in 1813, when his forces retook Caracas from troops loyal to Spain. After three years in exile he returned to fight and eventually won the war of liberation that led to the formation of an expansive Colombia, of which he became dictator until 1825. Thereafter, separatist movements created the independent states of Venezuela, Ecuador, Peru, and Bolivia. (Ann Ronan Picture Library)

colony's adherence, but in 1822, only a year after John finally returned to Portugal, his son Peter (Pedro) declared independence. Portuguese troops sent to reassert the Crown's authority in Brazil were defeated. Official recognition of the new South American republics by Britain and the United States soon followed, stimulated by economic motives, and opened a period of rising American commercial influence in Latin America which would in time replace Europe as the dominant influence in economic affairs from Mexico to Argentina.

Cost of the conflict

In the wider context of the Napoleonic Wars, the Peninsular War may be seen as having made an important contribution to the fall of the French Empire. It was not a mere backwater of the conflict, but a genuine second front which for seven years continually drained French manpower and matériel with a remarkably small military – though a very large subsidiary – commitment from Britain. The French, on the other hand, dispatched approximately 600,000 troops to the Peninsula in the course of the war, diverting considerable resources which would otherwise have been available to oppose other adversaries. They faced the paradox contained in an old saying whose truth was borne out yet again: 'In Spain a small army is beaten and a large one starves.'

Napoleon's Continental System proved personally disastrous, not least because it alienated his subservient and client states, thus providing Britain not only with moral support, particularly in the Mediterranean, but on a more tangible basis, with ready markets for the illegal trade in British and British colonial goods. Trade was vital to the British economy and by 1808 British merchants were suffering from the glut created by the French-imposed ban on the importation of British goods. The capture of French colonial possessions was not enough to alleviate the economic crisis in Britain; manufacturers of cloth and metalware needed regular and reliable foreign markets. The Peninsular War did much to solve their problems, for it led to the opening of the markets of the Spanish and Portuguese empires to British trade, leading to a rise in British exports from £8 million in 1805 to almost £20 million in 1809. The benefits of this trade were, moreover, to prove long-term, extending well into the twentieth century.

It is no easy matter to quantify precise numbers of casualties in this conflict. Records of battlefield losses and sick lists are generally available, though not always accurate: the war of attrition conducted by the guerrillas considerably complicates accurate tabulation of French and French allied losses. The average daily loss for France has been estimated at 100 men, or a total of nearly 240,000, and this in addition to the unquantifiable financial cost and strain that the war placed on the French treasury. Other estimates place French losses at 300,000. Apart from the cost of paying for and supporting his armies in Spain, Napoleon also provided huge loans to his brother Joseph, who, by the end of his reign in June 1813, had received a total of 620,000,000 reals. But in spite of such support he owed almost the same amount again to France by the end of the war. One estimate suggests a total cost to the French Empire of four billion reals (or in excess of a billion francs), not including all the cost of weapons and the other sinews of war. Such vast figures in human and financial resources alone demonstrate the important contribution that the Peninsular War played in bringing down Napoleonic rule in Europe. France could sustain a series of major campaigns on a single front; it patently could not on two, and in the wake of the disasters in Russia, Allied pressure ultimately proved too great a strain. The human cost of Britain's effort in the Peninsula is not known, but one aspect of the cost is fairly well documented: the financial support furnished in the form of massive subsidies of cash and huge quantities of arms, ammunition, and uniforms to Spain and Portugal. Between 1808 and 1814 Britain provided no less than £18 million in cash alone.

Ingredients of Allied success

The Peninsular War saw the rise of Britain's greatest general and, arguably, its greatest army. The high professional standards which the army achieved in Spain and Portugal were a testament to Wellington's abilities not only as a superb commander, but also as a highly skilled administrator. What qualities did he possess and how did they translate into success on the battlefield?

Wellington possessed remarkable stamina. He rose at 6.00 am and worked until midnight, writing large numbers of orders and dispatches, and riding between 30 and 50 miles (48 and 80 km) a day. In the six years he spent in the Peninsula he never once went on leave. His supreme self-confidence about his plans and his abilities was tempered by an understanding of his limitations based on clear-sighted forward planning and good use of intelligence. Wellington began the war with a clear and effective long-term strategy in mind and he adapted his tactics – usually but not always, defensive – to suit the ground, his opponents' strengths and weaknesses, and the capabilities of his men. He possessed the sort of intelligent mind that could quickly understand and assess a situation, whether at the strategic or tactical level. He laid his plans carefully and often anticipated those of his enemy. He had a good grasp of logistics and understood that an effective army required regular supplies of food, equipment, and ammunition. As such, he recognized the importance of an efficiently-run Commissariat.

Wellington seldom delegated authority to his subordinates in order to maintain personal control of affairs wherever possible, particularly on the battlefield. His orders were clear and he saw to it they were carried out precisely. While his failure to delegate may be seen as a fault, his consistent battlefield successes owed much to his presence on the scene, where by exposing himself to fire he encouraged his men and could see at first hand where action needed to be taken: sending reinforcements, exploiting a success, withdrawing, and so on. Proof of his constant presence in the thick of things is shown by his narrow escape from capture on three occasions and the three times when he was hit by musket balls – though without receiving serious injury. At Busaco Schaumann noted Wellington's conduct under fire: 'As usual, of course, Lord Wellington displayed extraordinary circumspection, calm, coolness and presence of mind. His orders were communicated in a loud voice and were short and precise.'

Wellington recognized – and acknowledged early in the war – that with only one army, and a small one at that, he could not afford to be defeated: he simply could not enjoy that luxury. Criticisms leveled against him as a strategically 'defensive' general should be analyzed in this light. He spent three years in a largely defensive posture and seldom took risks, fighting only when circumstances were favorable and then with positive results. By preventing the French from concentrating their massive numbers against him, he could fight their armies separately on reasonable terms and wait for the time to switch to the offensive. Thus, though the French had several hundred thousand men in the Peninsula at any given time, Wellington normally fought battles with about 50,000 men on each side. Napoleon's invasion of Russia in 1812 enabled him to do so, since that campaign not only required some French troops to transfer east, but would later deny to French commanders in the Peninsula much-needed reinforcements. From then on the French were obliged to fight a two-front war, thereby emboldening Wellington to move to the offensive. While it is true that at the tactical level he largely fought on the defensive, this was by no means always the case, as demonstrated at Oporto, Salamanca, Vitoria, and elsewhere.

Wellington also understood that the war would be long, and where other commanders might have regarded the odds as hopeless, he persisted. If his campaigns failed, he would accept responsibility, and he understood his dependence on the goodwill and cooperation of his hosts. 'I am convinced,' he declared to his superiors in London in October 1810,

that the honour and the interest of the country require us to remain here to the latest possible moment … I shall not seek to relieve myself of the burden of responsibility by causing the burden of defeat to rest upon the shoulders of ministers. I will not ask from them resources which they cannot spare … If the Portuguese do their duty, I can maintain myself here; if not, no effort in the power of Great Britain to make [war] will suffice to save Portugal.

He never gave in to what he called 'the croakers', officers in his own army who suggested, often behind the scenes, that the war was a lost cause, particularly in the period between Talavera and the withdrawal of Masséna from the Lines of Torres Vedras. Wellington inherited an army that, though it had undergone reforms under competent men like Abercromby and Moore, had a poor military record. Yet in the course of a few years he organized and trained the finest army of its size in Europe. And, whatever one may say about the contribution made by the Spanish soldiers and guerrillas, the balance of Allied victory or defeat in the Peninsula ultimately hung on the ability of Wellington's army to defeat the French in the field. This he did consistently with small numbers that usually varied between 30,000 and 60,000 men, of mixed nationality, but men of exceptionally high caliber, training, and leadership.

In short, Wellington's consistent victories owed much to his careful planning, his personal supervision of the fighting and his ability to react appropriately as circumstances changed. He anticipated the actions of his adversaries, who were often experienced generals, and so could plan accordingly. Finally, he commanded an army composed, in the main, of competent general officers and well-trained men, probably the best Britain has ever produced.

The setbacks at the Coa and at Burgos, though not battles in the usual sense of the word, show that British troops were not universally successful. In addition, operations in eastern Spain in 1813 led by Murray and Lord William Bentinck (1774–1839) met with lackluster results. Nor can it be said that the troops always conducted themselves with honor: their conduct after the fall of Badajoz and, to a lesser extent, San Sebastian, were nothing short of disgraceful, tarnishing what would otherwise have been a war waged by the British mostly on civilized terms. The fact that the government failed to provide Wellington with an adequate siege train only contributed to the huge losses and consequent desire of the men to run wild in the aftermath.

Wellington, who keenly appreciated the vital part played by logistics in war, wisely disrupted French supply lines wherever and whenever possible, while protecting his own. He also operated an extensive intelligence network, considerably facilitated by campaigning in friendly country, whereas, conversely, the French had virtually nothing in the way of reliable intelligence.

While the French were continuously dogged by severe problems of supply and communication, the British operated in friendly country and were, for the most part, well supplied by sea. Thus, while by its nature the war could only be won by operations conducted on land, the contribution made by the Royal Navy was absolutely vital to the success of its terrestrial arm by maintaining unrestricted communication and supply links with Britain. The French could only communicate via the Pyrenees and could neither supply their troops nor transport them by sea either in the Bay of Biscay or in the Mediterranean. The British, conversely, could operate with complete freedom at sea, and it was this extraordinary flexibility that enabled them not only to land an expeditionary force in Portugal in 1808, but also to be able, when circumstances demanded it, to withdraw it from Corunna in January 1809 and then to send another back to Portugal again in April. The relationship between sea power and the success of armies on land is often overlooked; the Peninsular War provides an excellent example of how sea power is not simply confined to great fleet actions. Having said this, only a great naval power like Britain

could enjoy such flexibility and it was won as a result of a great naval action, the victory of Trafalgar in 1805.

Allied success owed much, but not all, to Wellington. One can also trace it to Portugal and Spain's contribution to the war effort and to French mistakes and shortcomings. Beresford's reconstitution and reconstruction of the Portuguese army also made a significant contribution to Allied victory. So also did the extremely formidable system of strongpoints established to protect Lisbon. The Lines of Torres Vedras enabled Wellington to sit in complete security behind a defensive cordon, so protecting at least central and southern Portugal, and wait for the opportune time to project his forces into Spain.

One may easily dismiss the regular Spanish armies of 1808–1809 on the grounds of their poor performance, but if French losses at Bailen were easily replaceable, the reputation lost there could not be. The very existence of these armies, however easily they were shattered in 1808–1809, gave heart to many Spaniards, especially the guerrillas. In short, the Spanish armies, though consistently defeated and unreliable, were persistent and could never be completely discounted by the French. Their mere existence tied down large numbers of troops who otherwise would have concentrated against the much smaller British and Portuguese forces, who never numbered more than 60,000 men. Given the utterly inadequate transport and equipment, appalling training and acute shortage of cavalry horses, combined with a penurious rabble led by fools or worse, it is little wonder that the Spanish armies would consistently meet disaster in the field. Yet back they would come with a determination not seen elsewhere in Europe. It must be acknowledged, moreover, that toward the end of the war, after Wellington had assumed supreme command over the Spanish armies, the regular forces managed to raise their standards and acquitted themselves well at such actions as Vitoria and the siege of San Sebastian.

Although impossible to quantify by their very nature, and whether one condemns the combatants as savage brutes and murderers or brave patriot heroes (or perhaps a combination of the two), the impact of guerrilla operations must not be underestimated. These largely anonymous characters harried French communications throughout Portugal and Spain and tied down large numbers of men sent in usually fruitless attempts to exterminate them. In effect, the French were forced to fight on two fronts: against the regular Allied armies in the field and against the Spanish, and, to a lesser degree, the Portuguese guerrillas along their flanks and in their rear. Communications and supply lines could be severed sometimes at will and the geography of the countryside proved ideal for guerrilla operations. Apart from the actual combatants, unarmed civilians often paid the price, marking the Peninsular War out from all other conflicts since the seventeenth century as the most vicious and comprehensive in its impact on civilian life. The military consequences were significant: unremitting guerrilla operations not only sapped French strength, but the cost to morale was very great as well. In short, without the support and contributions to the war effort made by Spain and Portugal, as he himself acknowledged after 1814, Wellington could not have won the war.

The contributions of Spain and Portugal, combined with the ever-present guerrillas, and, of course, the British Army itself, rendered the French strategy of concentrating superior forces against a critical point in search of a decisive result much less feasible. True, the French enjoyed overall numerical superiority, but they were seldom able to profit from this advantage. To concentrate they had to abandon large areas to their enemy, only to have to seize them back later. Their numbers were dissipated in a hopeless attempt to keep the population under control, supply lines open and to garrison towns and cities. Perhaps the greatest miscalculation made by France was her failure to recognize the hostility felt by the Iberian people. Trying to subjugate a hostile civilian population while simultaneously taking on the Allied army proved too much. As Wellington himself stated:

It is true that [the French defeat in Spain] may in part be attributed to the operations of the allied armies in the Peninsula; but a great proportion of it must be ascribed to the enmity of the people of Spain. I have known of not less than 380,000 men of the French army in Spain at one moment & yet with no authority beyond the spot where they stood

The French themselves admitted there was no military solution to civilian animosity. Recalling his days as provincial Governor-General of Catalonia 1810–1811, Marshal Macdonald described the problem with telling succinctness: 'The enemy were ubiquitous, and yet I could find them nowhere, though I travelled the length and breadth of the province.'

Traditional French methods of supply failed completely in the Peninsula. Campaigning in the rich and fertile Po and Danube Valleys was not the same as in East Prussia and Poland, as Napoleon had discovered in 1807, and Spain and Portugal were even worse, exacerbated by 'scorched earth'. Here, 'living off the land' alone proved impossible, making supply at best tenuous and at worst an insupportable problem in an intensely hostile and geographically inhospitable land. In compelling subservient peoples to support them, the French opened a Pandora's box.

In contrast to Wellington's exceptional leadership qualities, French commanders, though often excellent men, such as Junot, Victor, Masséna, Marmont, and Soult, were at times their own worst enemies, acting out of motives of jealousy, mistrust, and professional rivalry in competition for independent success. The net result was painfully predictable: consistent and sometimes disastrous failure to cooperate with one another in a war where their combined numerical superiority could have been tapped with success and in a country where communication was already nearly impossible owing to the ubiquitous guerrilla presence.

Much credit is due to Welllington for persuading his government to continue the war even after the disastrous evacuation of Moore's army from Spain. Not only did Wellington recognize that he could hold Portugal with a relatively small force in conjunction with a reorganized Portuguese army, he appreciated the tenuous nature of France's occupation of Spain. Its sheer size and the scale of popular hostility to the occupier meant that France could probably never completely subjugate the country. In a land where the population already lived at subsistence levels, it was hopeless, despite the most draconian methods, to try to supply armies that totaled hundreds of thousands. To cope with this intractable problem, French lines of communication had necessarily to become overstretched, leaving them extremely vulnerable to guerrilla attacks. Those who claim that the war was unwinnable from the outset can do so only with the safety of hindsight, but it is clear that the French faced daunting obstacles from the moment the Spanish people rose up – and still more when Wellesley arrived in Portugal a few months later.

However daunting the obstacles appeared at the outset of the war – poor supply, uneven leadership at senior levels, varied and often times harsh climate and terrain, and great distances – Napoleon remained largely oblivious to the challenge that loomed ahead. Perhaps he had good reason for viewing his prospects optimistically: after all, when Junot marched into Portugal in 1807, France had no other active fronts competing for men and the veterans of the campaigns of 1805–1807 were not even required for the occupation; they could remain in the cantonments on the Rhine, the Elbe, and the Oder. Neither the scale nor the determination of Spanish resistance were initially clear, and even after all these obstacles became obvious, including Britain's inevitable intervention, Napoleon continued to prosecute the war, and his ardor never faded. Of course it may be argued with some justice that it was precisely this miscalculation and his self-deluding bravado that cost Napoleon the war, yet only with hindsight does the victory won by the Allies seem a foregone conclusion. It could easily have been different for, even when Britain did intervene, there were many, not just the 'croakers' in Wellington's army but also those on the Opposition benches in Parliament, who, in the wake of Corunna and at various other critical moments in the war, advocated withdrawal from the Peninsula.

It must also be stressed that, even when Britain continued her efforts, it was not until 1812, with the diversion of French troops to the Russian front, that Wellington could hope to undertake a full-scale invasion of Spain. Any time before that period a major battlefield defeat might have spelled the end of Britain's commitment to her Iberian allies. This was the reality of a country with only one army to lose and governments that depended on parliamentary support for survival. This was never the case with Napoleonic France, which, in spite of consistent setbacks and the realization that Spain could never be subjugated, stubbornly continued to maintain her hold on Spain until forcibly driven out.

The War in the Peninsula enabled the British Army to share in the overall Allied effort against Napoleonic France, not simply to be left to diversionary operations as in the past. For the first time in a century a major British force, much larger than in the wars of the mid-eighteenth century, could operate on the European mainland. The army won a series of unbroken victories in the field and, apart from Burgos, succeeded in every assault on a fortified position. Almost every regiment in the army earned some share of glory in the Peninsula, as is shown by the battle honors which adorn their regimental colors even today.

Thus, when the Allied powers sat down to conclude the Treaty of Paris in 1814, Britain's major contribution to the defeat of France was more than acknowledged by the other Great Powers. Had Britain confined her war effort to the supply (large though it was) of subsidies and naval operations alone, her influence at the peace conferences which followed Napoleon's first and second abdications would never have been so considerable as it ultimately proved to be. Whether his empire and dynasty would have survived had Napoleon never embarked on his Iberian adventure is open to debate, but clearly his decision to do so, and Britain's determination to press on for final victory, contributed materially to his ultimate downfall.

Further reading

Literature relating to the Peninsular War, both primary and secondary, is very large. The following selection represents some of the works that will provide a broad cross-section of material on the subject. Many primary sources have recently been reprinted.

Secondary Sources

Alexander, Don, *Rod of Iron: French Counterinsurgency Policy in Aragon during the Peninsular War*, Wilmington, Del., Scholarly Resources, 1985.

Brett-James, Anthony, *Life in Wellington's Army*, London, Allen and Unwin, 1972.

Chartrand, René, *Bussaco 1810*, Oxford, Osprey Publishing, 2001.

– *Vimeiro 1808*, Oxford, Osprey Publishing, 2001.

Davies, David, *Sir John Moore's Peninsular Campaign, 1808–1809*, The Hague, M. Nijhoff, 1974.

Esdaile, Charles, *The Spanish Army in the Peninsular War*, Manchester, Manchester University Press, 1988.

– *The Duke of Wellington and the Command of the Spanish Army, 1812–14*, Houndmills, Basingstoke, Hampshire, Macmillan, 1990.

Fletcher, Ian, et. al., *Aspects of the Struggle for the Iberian Peninsula*, Staplehurst, Kent, Spellmount Publishing, 1998.

Fletcher, Ian, *Badajoz 1812*, Oxford, Osprey Publishing, 1999.

– *Bloody Albuera: The 1811 Campaign in the Peninsula*, Crowood Press, 2001.

– *Galloping at Everything: The British Cavalry in the Peninsular War and at Waterloo, 1808–15*, Staplehurst, Kent, Spellmount Publishing, 2001.

– *Salamanca 1812*, Oxford, Osprey Publishing, 1997.

– *Vittoria 1813*, Oxford, Osprey Publishing, 1998.

Fortescue, Sir John, *History of the British Army*, 13 vols., London, Macmillan, 1910–1930.

Gates, David, *The Spanish Ulcer: A History of the Peninsular War*, London, W. W. Norton & Co., 1986; repr, 2001.

Glover, Michael, *Legacy of Glory: The Bonaparte Kingdom of Spain*, New York, Charles Scribner, 1971.

– *The Peninsular War, 1807-14: A Concise Military History*, Newton Abbot, David & Charles, 1974.

– *Wellington's Army in the Peninsula, 1808-1814*, New York, Hippocrene Books, 1977.

– *Wellington as Military Commander*, London, Batsford, 1968.

– *Wellington's Peninsular Victories*, London, Batsford,1963.

Grehan, John, *The Lines of Torres Vedras: The Cornerstone of Wellington's Strategy in the Peninsular War, 1809-1812*, Staplehurst, Spellmount Press, 2000.

Griffith, Paddy, ed., *A History of the Peninsular War: Modern Studies of the War in Spain and Portugal, 1808-1814*, London, Greenhill Books, 1999.

Griffith, Paddy, *Wellington Commander*, Chichester, Sussex, Anthony Bird, 1985.

Guedalla, Philip, *The Duke*, London, Hodder & Stoughton,1931.

Haythornthwaite, Philip, *The Armies of Wellington*, London, Arms and Armour Press, 1994.

– *Corunna 1809*, Oxford, Osprey Publishing, 2001.

– *Uniforms of the Peninsular War*, Blandford Press, Poole, Dorset, 1978.

Hibbert, Christopher, *Corunna*, New York, Macmillan, 1961.

Humble, Richard, *Napoleon's Peninsular Marshals*, London, Purcell Book Services, 1973.

Lachouque, Henri, Tranié, Jean and Carmigniani, J-C., *Napoleon's War in Spain*, London, Arms and Armour Press, 1982.

Longford, Elizabeth, *Wellington: The Years of the Sword*, New York, Harper & Row, 1969; repr. 1985.

Lovett, Gabriel, *Napoleon and the Birth of Modern Spain*, 2 vols, New York, NYU Press, 1965.

Myatt, Frederick, *British Sieges in the Peninsular War*, Tunbridge Wells, Spellmount Press, 1987.

Napier, William, *A History of the War in the Peninsula and the South of France, 1807–1814*, 6 vols., London, T & W Boone, 1832–40; repr. 1993.

Oman, Sir Charles, *A History of the Peninsular War*, 7 vols. Oxford, Oxford University Press, 1902–30; repr. 1996.

Paget, Julian, *Wellington's Peninsular War*, London, Leo Cooper, 1990.

Parkinson, Roger, *The Peninsular War*, London, Granada, 1973; repr. 2000.

Rudorff, R., *War to the Death: the Sieges of Saragossa*, London, Hamish Hamilton, 1974.

Tone, John, *The Fatal Knot: The Guerrilla War in Navarre and the Defeat of Napoleon in Spain*, Chapel Hill, University of North Carolina Press, 1994.

Weller, Jac, *Wellington in the Peninsula*, London, N. Vane, 1962, repr. 1992.

Published Dispatches, Memoirs and Eyewitness Accounts

Boutflower, Charles, *The Journal of an Army Surgeon during the Peninsular War*, New York, De Capo Press, 1997.

Bragge, William, *Peninsular Portrait, 1811–1814: The Letters of Capt. W. Bragge, Third (King's Own) Dragoons*, ed., S. A. Cassels, London, Oxford University Press, 1963.

Costello, Edward, *Adventures of a Soldier: The Peninsular and Waterloo Campaigns*, ed., Antony Brett-James, London, Longmans, 1967.

Fletcher, Ian, ed., *Voices from the Peninsula: Eyewitness Accounts by Soldiers of Wellington's Army, 1808–1814*, London, Greenhill Books, 2001.

Harris, John, *Recollections of Rifleman Harris*, London, 1848.; repr. Hamden,Conn, Archon Books, 1970.

Larpent, F. Seymour, *Private Journal of F. Seymour Larpent, Judge-AdvocateGeneral*, London, R. Bentley, 1853; repr. 2001.

Pelet, Jean Jacques, *The French Campaign in Portugal, 1810–1811: An Account*, ed. and trans., Donald Horward, Minneapolis, University of Minnesota Press, 1973.

Rathbone, Julian, *Wellington's War: Peninsular Dispatches presented by Julian Rathbone*, London, Michael Joseph, 1984.

Schaumann, A. L. F., *On the Road with Wellington: The Diary of a War Commissary*, London, Greenhill Books, 1999.

Simmons, George, *A British Rifleman: The Journals and Correspondence of Major George Simmons, Rifle Brigade*, London, A & C Black, 1899.

Suchet, Louis-Gabriel, *Memoirs of the War in Spain*, London, H. Colburn, 1829.

Tomkinson, Lt.-Col. William, *The Diary of a Cavalry Officer in the Peninsular and Waterloo Campaigns, 1809–1815*, London, S. Sonnenschein & Co, 1894; repr. 2000.

von Brandt, Heinrich, *In the Legions of Napoleon: The Memoirs of a Polish Officer in Spain and Russia, 1808–1813*, trans. and ed., Jonathan North, London, Greenhill Books, 1999.

Wellington, Duke of, *Supplementary Dispatches and Memoranda*, 15 vols., ed., his son, London, John Murray, 1858-72.

– *Dispatches of Field Marshal the Duke of Wellington*, ed., Col. J. Gurwood, 8 vols., London, Parker, Furnivall & Parker, 1844; repr. Millwood NY, Kraus Reprint Co., 1973.

Wheatley, Edmund, *The Wheatley Diary*, ed., Christopher Hibbert, London, Longmans, 1964.

Wheeler, W., *The Letters of Private Wheeler, 1809–28*, ed., B. H. Liddell-Hart, Boston, Houghton Mifflin, 1951.

Index

Other titles in the Essential Histories series

The Crusades
ISBN 1 84176 179 6

The Crimean War
ISBN 1 84176 186 9

**The Seven Years'
War**
ISBN 1 84176 191 5

**The Napoleonic
Wars (1)** The rise of
the Emperor 1805–1807
ISBN 1 84176 205 9

**The Napoleonic
Wars (2)** The empires
fight back 1808–1812
ISBN 1 84176 298 9

**The French
Revolutionary Wars**
ISBN 1 84176 283 0

**Campaigns of the
Norman Conquest**
ISBN 1 84176 228 8

**The American Civil
War (1)** The war in the
East 1861–May 1863
ISBN 1 84176 239 3

**The American Civil
War (2)** The war in the
West 1861–July 1863
ISBN 1 84176 240 7

**The American Civil
War (3)** The war in the
East 1863–1865
ISBN 1 84176 241 5

**The American Civil
War (4)** The war in the
West 1863–1865
ISBN 1 84176 242 3

The Korean War
ISBN 1 84176 282 2

**The First World War
(1)** The Eastern Front
1914–1918
ISBN 1 84176 342 X

**The First World War
(2)** The Western Front
1914–1916
ISBN 1 84176 347 0

**The Punic Wars
264–146 BC**
ISBN 1 84176 355 1

**The Falklands
War 1982**
ISBN 1 84176 422 1

**The Napoleonic Wars
(3)** The Peninsular War
1807–1814
ISBN 1 84176 370 5

**The Second World
War (1)** The Pacific
ISBN 1 84176 229 6

**The Iran-Iraq War
1980–1988**
ISBN 1 84176 371 3
April 2002

**The French Religious
Wars 1562–1598**
ISBN 1 84176 395 0
June 2002

**The First World War
(3)** The Western Front
1916–1918
ISBN 1 84176 348 9
June 2002

**The First World War
(4)** The Mediterranean
Front 1914–1923
ISBN 1 84176 373 X
July 2002

**The Second World
War (2)** The Eastern
Front 1941–1945
ISBN 1 84176 391 8
July 2002

**The Mexican War
1846–1848**
ISBN 1 84176 472 8
July 2002

**The Wars of
Alexander the Great**
ISBN 1 84176 473 6
July 2002

Praise for Essential Histories

'clear and concise' *History Today*

'an excellent series' *Military Illustrated*

'Osprey must be congratulated on Essential Histories' *Soldier*

'very useful, factual and educational' *Reference Reviews*

'valuable as an introduction for students or younger readers … older readers will also find something 'essential'
to their understanding' *Star Banner*

'accessible and well illustrated…' *Daily Express*

'… clearly written …' *Oxford Times*

'they make the perfect starting point for readers of any age' *Daily Mail*